A Walk
on the
Wild Side

by

Frederick Western

Pen and ink drawings by the author

authorHOUSE®

AuthorHouse™ UK Ltd.
500 Avebury Boulevard
Central Milton Keynes, MK9 2BE
www.authorhouse.co.uk
Phone: 08001974150

First published by AuthorHouse 12/8/2008

ISBN: 978-1-4343-9647-1 (sc)
ISBN: 978-1-4343-9648-8 (hc)

Printed in the United States of America
Bloomington, Indiana

This book is printed on acid-free paper.

CONTENTS

Foreword

"I'd like to go up to the Scottish Highlands on holiday this year, to see the place where Gavin Maxwell wrote his books". This was the single statement by my wife that changed our lives forever and with great trepidation I agreed.

We travelled up from Hampshire to London to join the Motorail, which took us overnight to Edinburgh and then north-west to Stirling and onwards to Fort William. It was at Spean Bridge a few miles further on that we had to stop and buy a couple of thick sweaters at the local woollen mill because there was snow even on the lower ground and it was freezing. I could not believe that this was the flaming month of June. We were from the south of England and this type of weather at this time of year was alien to us and our wardrobe we had brought with us reflected this.

Further shocks to the system were forthcoming when we were nearing our final destination. The small road over the hill of Mam Ratagan to Glenelg was then not as it is today. As the car edged its way up the single-track road with its tight bends, sheer drops and narrow bridges over deep crevices, we were beginning to wonder whether this was a good idea. The road was far too narrow to turn back so we had no option but to continue. Approaching the summit there was a very sharp bend followed immediately by an extremely steep incline which my car just about negotiated, for I had run out of lower gears. The trial of the climb was instantly forgotten when the summit car park was reached. The view of the Five Sisters of Kintail stretching out from Glen Shiel to the head of Loch Duich was magnificent.

We thought it couldn't get any better but visiting the place where Gavin Maxwell wrote his books was emotionally draining. Apart from the house, which had been burnt down, bulldozed and subsequently covered with sand over time, everything was as it had been described in his books. Adorned with flowers and shells from admiring visitors like ourselves was the cairn, where 'Edal' one of his otters had been laid to rest after dying in the fire - the waterfall where Maxwell said his ghost would return after his death - even the trailer used to cradle his boat the 'Polar Star' was lying in the overgrown walled garden rusting with the passage of time. Naturally the panoramic landscape had not changed – the old croft in the bay, half surrounded by the ring of bright water and the small islands with their coral beaches stretching out to the unmanned lighthouse were still part of the magical scene. The only addition to times gone by was the large boulder placed where Maxwell's writing desk had been, which now rested above the casket containing his ashes.

Little did we know we would fall in love with Glenelg and the surrounding area of the Kyle of Lochalsh so much that annual holidays just weren't enough. The move to Glenelg and subsequently to Ardgay and the reasons for this are described in more detail in the following chapter.

The regions of Wester Ross and Sutherland could not be more different as Sutherland has a more varied range of habitats and therefore a wider variety of birds and wildlife, which is more akin to our interests. All this coupled with a better climate made Sutherland the place for us and so began sixteen years of discovery.

Chapter 1

HOME SWEET HOME

PINE MARTEN

My love affair with the Scottish Highlands started way back in 1974 when, after a lot of persuading by my wife, we headed north on our annual summer holiday.

The previous year my wife had received the trilogy of books written by Gavin Maxwell (Ring of Bright Water, The Rocks Remain and Raven Seek Thy Brother) as a leaving present from fellow employees where she worked in central London. These books affected her so much that she had to see for herself the area where Maxwell lived and wrote these famous manuscripts, even though the house had been burnt to the ground and Maxwell himself had long since died. Reluctantly I agreed and so began a series of events that changed our lives.

After an arduous overnight journey by Motorail from London to Edinburgh, the drive to the west Highland coast was in total contrast. Through the rolling Perthshire hills; past the spectacular Three Sisters of atmospheric Glencoe; to Fort William, where snow capped Ben Nevis crept from behind a cloud; through Glenshiel, guarded by the magnificent Five Sisters of Kintail, and finally over Mam Ratagan to the small village of Glenelg - I was hooked. We spent every annual holiday for the next six years in the Highlands, touring for part of the time but always returning to Glenelg and Sandaig (or Camusfearna as Maxwell called it) before returning south. It was during one of these trips that we heard that some land was for sale on the outskirts of the village and after many trials and tribulations we eventually purchased one of the building plots - our own little bit of the Highlands. Two years of arduous saving with no holidays and selling our property in southern England (Hampshire) enabled us to arrange to have a bungalow built on our half an acre of very rough pasture and rushes.

We travelled north in June 1982 with an old military lightweight Land Rover pulling a second hand caravan that we intended living in until the bungalow was completed. With our furniture in storage, the caravan containing essential equipment and our two cats bestowed in the Land Rover, we began our adventure. We moved into the bungalow in November of that year with the intention of supplying bed and breakfast accommodation to the steady flow of tourists that visited this picturesque area. After two horrendous winters and one summer of tourists we realised that visiting a place on holiday and living there were two entirely different propositions. Apart from the weather, where gales and horizontal rain seemed to rage continuously from September to May, we decided that you either liked or hated sharing your home with paying guests - we hated it.

It was while we were reluctantly trying to resurrect our careers and return south that a friend who we knew from our time in Hampshire, who was now living in Bonar Bridge in Sutherland, invited us to visit her for the day. Bonar Bridge is situated in the north-east of Highland Region nestling on the shores of the Kyle of Sutherland, some 115 miles from Glenelg. Our journey across to the eastern side of the Highlands was both interesting and rewarding. After passing through Inverness, the Highland capital, there was a distinct contrast between the rugged west coast and the more gentle and softer eastern side of Ross-shire. The undulating heather moor and mountain giving way to fenced green fields of the Black Isle, very like parts of northern England. Once over the border into Sutherland the landscape changed once more into somewhere in between. Our knowledge of Sutherland was limited to a couple of touring holidays many years ago to the north-west coasts where the only recollection was one of continuous peat bog punctuated with the odd mountain or two.

After a quick reconnoitre of the coastal fringe from Bonar Bridge to Golspie, followed by an informative lunch on the varied habitats, nature reserves, climate and wildlife to be seen in the area we became increasingly interested in the possibility of a move to a county we hadn't even considered beforehand. Two of the many attractive features of the area were its diverse habitats of mountain and moor, coastal estuaries, rugged coastline and mixed woodland, all within a radius of thirty miles and the easy accessibility to our beloved west coast. On our return to Glenelg we stopped off at the estate agents in Inverness to pick up some information on properties for sale in the immediate vicinity of Bonar Bridge.

During our visit with our friend we had jokingly listed our preferred requirements of the property we would like which consisted of:- three bedroomed traditional building with outbuildings, relatively sheltered, situated on a track, a pond for our ducks and surrounded by mature trees. Would you believe it, within a week we had a telephone call to say that a property with our exact specifications was for sale in Ardgay, which is a small village situated just a mile from Bonar Bridge on the other side of the stretch of water known as the Kyle of Sutherland. Unfortunately when I rang the seller the property had been sold, but only verbally. I asked if he would inform us if the deal fell through and sure enough a week later he rang. We hastily arranged to view and made tracks north-east the next day.

Following his directions we left the village on a single-track road, through a closed farm gate to the end of a metalled road and on to a rough track with a centre strip of short-cropped grass and heather. The winding track descended gradually through an avenue of birch, willow, Scots pine and juniper bushes to end at a three bar wooden gate hung between two stone pillars. As we parked in the driveway a cursory glance revealed that we had found our shangri-la. On one side of the drive a small grass area led into a mixed woodland copse, which ran down to a large stone barn with a corrugated roof, whilst the other side had the same grassy margin but with a small burn (stream) that separated it from a further small broadleaf copse. This burn tumbled over a couple of natural stone waterfalls at the head of two small pools before running under a wooden planked bridge to emerge into a main pond. This natural pond was about sixty feet by twenty feet with a small grass covered island at one end bedecked with willow scrub and a stunted Scots pine. The easterly view from the garden was breathtaking, stretching from the adjacent field over the purple tinged birch woodland of early spring to the Inner Dornoch Firth and the Migdale hills beyond. The house appeared to be a former croft house that had been extended both ways to form an 'L' shaped property incorporating an integral garage. Once past the formalities an in-depth guided tour revealed its inner secrets. Once a half-house, that is one room upstairs and one down, it had been extended many moons ago to produce a normal Highland croft house of two bedrooms in the loft space and two living rooms downstairs. Further extensions and modernisations had increased the size to include another bedroom, an improved bathroom and kitchen with an additional garage and sun lounge that overlooked that magnificent easterly view. Pine panelling was everywhere from the original croft ceiling in the dining room through to the hall, staircase and lounge, where during a welcoming coffee in front of a roaring wood burning stove the property's interesting past was revealed.

The croft had been in the Munro-Rattray family for at least a hundred years but its history before the early 1880's is unfortunately not known. Donald Munro was succeeded in his tenancy from the Estate by his nephew Hugh Munro, who was, in turn succeeded by his daughter's husband Robert Rattray. The Rattray's continued to work the croft until their retirement in 1967 when it was sold to the well-known British actor James Robertson Justice in the name of his companion Baroness von Meyendoff. He kept the property to indulge in his passion of falconry on the adjoining moors. It changed hands again a couple of times up until the present day. Ironically before the purchase of this house James Robertson Justice formerly owned Spinningdale House, which is situated on the other side of the Inner Dornoch Firth. It was invariably full of guests when he was at home including Phillip Glasier (the well known falconer), Prince Philip, a young Prince Charles and Gavin Maxwell, to name but a few. It seemed the Maxwell connection had to be continued and we immediately put in a bid for the house we had fallen in love with at first sight.

After some haggling our offer was finally accepted provide we could sell our property in Glenelg, which was not going to be easy because of the remote location and the asking price which ruled out a holiday home. A few weeks passed and potential buyers from near and far came and went, then fate took control. I am a firm believer that your destiny is pre-arranged but during your life crossroads appear and it is your choice which road you follow. My destiny appeared in the shape of the local district nurse from the village who suddenly required a larger house to accommodate herself and her recently widowed mother, who had just sold her house in Edinburgh. A deal was struck and preparations were made to move to our dream house where we finally arrived in July 1984.

Our introduction to the local wildlife began at once as the resident swallows, which were nesting in the barn, took immediate objection to our three cats. Every time the cats were in the vicinity of the barn the two adult swallows, as if by telepathy, shot out through the top of the opened stable door and dive bombed the unsuspecting moggies. Just like German Stuka's (world war II aircraft) they would climb to gain height, then descend at a great speed and "chit" as they passed within inches of the cats' heads before climbing again for a repeat performance. Sam, our large black male, took exception to this and proceeded to launch himself into the air trying to catch these irritant large flies as they passed by, typical Sam! Apart from Sam and a female tabby, Brandy (our two cats that had travelled from Hampshire with us) we now had an additional cat, three ducks and a drake, which we had acquired at Glenelg. I should perhaps say Emma, the small black female kitten, had acquired us. She appeared quite suddenly early one morning playing with Brandy around a log pile at the back of the caravan. She was about ten weeks old and had only just left her mother and was obviously very hungry as she constantly chewed small pieces of wood as if it was food. Thinking cat food might be too rich for her system, we placed some left-over porridge from breakfast in a saucer, which she ate with relish. After that she was sitting outside the caravan door every morning like a little waif and stray, which she was of course, waiting for her porridge and milk. Her timing was impeccable, as we got up she was there, it was then that we discovered how. She had been sleeping at night underneath the caravan in the well of the spare wheel and therefore could hear us arise. As the nights began to get colder we eventually coaxed her inside where she subsequently became part of the family. The ducks, which were a friend's surplus stock, were originally just to supply us with eggs but also as their individual characters began to show through they too became more than just livestock.

As well as the swallows other members of the family (house

martins and sand martins) have visited the garden on calm summer days, swooping high over the pond to catch the rising insects and disappearing as quickly as they arrived. The pond attracts a wide variety of bird life, especially wild mallards who upon seeing our domesticated ducks swimming around unmolested, tumble out of the sky before water ski-ing to a halt. They are invariably in pairs and it is not until the two species are together side by side that the difference in size is apparent. The wild varieties are so much smaller and more compact with the female's plumage especially being particularly bright and defined. The mallard, being the most familiar duck in the British Isles is treated with a very blasé attitude, much in common with the house sparrow, starling and chaffinch etc., which does not do justice to their detailed intricate plumage, which is so apparent when carefully studied. The male's glossy green head, white collar and maroon breast, coupled with the female's delicate brown plumage and striking blue wing patch, make them a very handsome pair to adorn any pond. A further but unwelcome visitor to the pond, by the ducks at least, is the large conspicuous grey heron. The first indication that a heron, or for that matter a bird of prey is around, is the sudden realisation of acute panic instilled in the ducks as they fly from all parts of the garden into the sanctity of the pond. It is the sheer size of this huge winged predator as it descends to land gently at the waters edge that creates unnecessary fear, for neither heron or raptor has attempted to prey on the ducks at any time even when they were ducklings and a mere mouthful. The heron is an expert fisherman and is able to extend his neck in an instant to grab any unsuspecting fish that might swim within range of his long, dagger-like bill. As there are no fish in the pond this visitor quickly turns his attentions to the numerous amount of frogs that inhabit the marshy areas of the garden that border the watercourses. Though generally solitary hunters, herons breed gregariously in colonies, usually building in the high tops of large trees using the same nest year after year resulting in a nest several feet across. Due to a lack of large trees on the north coast of Sutherland the herons there breed on cliff faces, with the nests consisting of a jumble of sticks and jetsam sitting precariously on small ledges above the deep blue sea.

11

Apart from the dapper little common pied wagtail, an infrequent but regular visitor to the pond has been his close relative, the grey wagtail. Not to be confused with the yellow wagtail that is a summer visitor to England and very rare in Scotland, this elegant little black, grey and yellow bird often walks along the waters edge, perches on an exposed boulder with his long tail twitching up and down watching for insects. Although the grey wagtail is an unusual garden bird, the common sandpiper, which has appeared on a couple of occasions, is unheard of. I can only assume that both these birds had strayed from the river where they breed, which is not two hundred yards from the garden.

Being somewhat remote and because of the continuous supply of peanuts and seed, the garden is full of birds all year round. From the more common chaffinch, blue tit, great tit, coal tit and greenfinch, which are the favourite prey of the local sparrowhawk, through to the more unusual great-spotted woodpecker and Scottish crossbill to the positively exotic winter visiting waxwings. Sightings of waxwings are usually infrequent in Britain but every few years, due to high populations and a failure of their favourite food crop (the rowan berry), they appear in large numbers from their breeding grounds in northern Scandinavia. These extremely attractive birds are very gregarious and flock together to feed on the berries of a variety of shrubs. One year about half a dozen appeared in the garden on a bright December day to subsequently strip the remaining fruit from the cotoneaster bushes. What an attractive sight they made, generally pinkish brown in colour with a black chin and eye stripe leading to a swept-back crest. The bright black wings are marked with red white and yellow and the black-banded tail has a yellow tip. The bird gets its name from the unusual waxy looking red tips to the upper flight feathers.

With the very varied habitats that surround our property a vast array of raptors either visit or breed in the near vicinity. Buzzard, kestrel and sparrowhawk nest in the surrounding mixed woodlands and hen harrier, peregrine and the occasional osprey and golden eagle can be seen patrolling the open moorland that backs onto the garden, stretching to the foothills of Carn Bhren at 2000ft and beyond. On three occasions young male sparrowhawks have flown into the sun lounge windows despite us having taken the precaution of plastering the glass with bird silhouettes. Unfortunately one broke his neck but the others survived. One I found lying prostrate, his body being supported by the branches of some dwarf conifers that were just below the point of impact that was highlighted by wing impressions embossed on the glass. To my astonishment he was still alive so I held the limp body tight in my hands so that the warmth would help relieve the shock. After a few minutes the casualty began to come round and rewarded my kindness by struggling violently and sinking his extremely sharp talons into my hand. Pleased that he had recovered I placed him on a low branch of one of our crab apple trees. After spending several minutes looking around and getting his bearings he flew off across the adjoining field and into the bordering woodland, no doubt helped on his way by one of our inquisitive cats that had arrived on the scene. He obviously survived as an hour later he was back pursuing chaffinches around the garden conspicuous by his ruffled head and chest feathers.

The other casualty was not so fortunate. I found him entangled along with his quarry, a chaffinch again, in a solitary rose bush that was beneath the window where they both hit. After carefully freeing him from the entrapping thorns and inspecting for obvious damage, I released him but he could only fly a short distance before crash landing. Although surprisingly quick on his feet, I caught him and placed him in an old rabbit hutch and run that I had kept for such occasions. As he sat there quietly on a rapidly constructed perch I could see one wing was hanging slightly lower than the other. Having not the appropriate authority or the knowledge to treat this bird I telephoned a local licensed raptor keeper who helps and treats many raptors that have had accidents or are victims of poisonings. He works in close contact with the RSPB and due to his falconry expertise hacks back to the wild many young and recovered birds. He needed to see the sparrowhawk to assess the damage and evaluate the problems, as sparrowhawks are particularly difficult to treat successfully, so I made arrangements to travel the following morning as by this time it was getting late. After spending a comfortable night (the bird not me), I transferred him to a cardboard box and my wife and I travelled the twenty-five miles to await the verdict. As I thought it was a broken wing, not a bad break but one that he would need a large amount of luck for it to mend correctly and regain complete mobility in the wing to enable him to return to the wild. After strapping up the wing and placing him in a holding cage it was agreed that I would telephone in a couple of weeks to see what progress had been made.

After a very welcome cup of coffee we were offered a guided tour of the enclosures that contained a variety of raptors in various degrees of rehabilitation. Most of the wild birds were young buzzards with an array of injuries resulting from flying into electricity pylons and others recovering from indiscriminate poisonings. Although the ability to study the buzzard from close quarters was indeed fascinating the sight of the two birds perched on blocks in different parts of the garden, for obvious reasons, was an experience to be remembered. One was the keeper's own captive bred peregrine and the other a truly wild ex-falconry goshawk due to be shortly given her freedom. This peregrine was screaming (as only peregrines can) for her morning bath, as captive birds especially like to bathe and then preen to keep their feathers in pristine condition. I have been fortunate to see many peregrines in the wild, usually at a distance, either at a nest or just flying over the open moor but this was different. Falconers prefer females because they are larger and better hunters and this scimitar-winged assassin was every inch a killer, from her needle sharp talons to her formidable hooked beak. As I approached she stopped screaming. Hunched and alert perched on her block, she watched my every movement with that large dark brown eye concealed by a black moustachial streak. Now quiet and reserved it was difficult to imagine that this blue-black beauty was the ultimate flying machine, capable of the infamous spectacular plunge (stoop) performed at breathtaking speed to kill cleanly and instantly by breaking the neck of the unfortunate victim with the claw of the hind toe.

In contrast the female goshawk was a real spitfire trying to fly at these unwelcome intruders but being checked by the leash (leather throng), which is used to tether a hawk to its block. After gentle stroking of the breast and some reassuring noises made by the keeper she began to calm down. She was much larger and a more powerful version of the sparrowhawk I had just brought in. Roughly about the same size as a buzzard, with a distinctive whitish streak running from the eyebrow to the ear coverts that masked her piercing yellow eye which never missed a thing. This magnificent bird, which has been severely persecuted by those concerned with game preservation, has a normal diet of mainly wood pigeons, the crow family and rabbits, which are themselves considered pests. The goshawk, although still a very rare breeding species in Britain, has built up its numbers in some areas due to escapee's from falconry and deliberate introductions, like this one. Some time later I telephoned the raptor keeper to find out how my sparrowhawk had fared and was delighted to hear that the wing had healed and he had been successfully released.

For a good few years after we first moved into the house a pair of hen harriers used to appear over the tops of the adjoining Scots pine trees on a regular basis but since the conifer plantations over the river have begun to grow they gradually disappeared. Whenever the peregrine pays us a visit you can be sure feathers will fly. On one such occasion over the field in front of the house a peregrine continually dive-bombed a flock of mistle thrushes that were feeding on insects attracted to newly created cow-pats. I am sure this was merely mischievousness rather than serious intent but the next episode certainly was deadly serious. As I was walking down the track one morning towards our front gate admiring the view I noticed a bird climbing high in the sky then levelling out. Suddenly with wings folded back the bird descended rapidly like an arrow, cutting across the moor towards the river before disappearing behind a group of birch trees lying in a natural valley (the famous stoop). At the same time two portly wood pigeons flapped into action by diving into the nearest cover available, but no peregrine. I decided to investigate. After negotiating the heather I carefully crept into the boggy gully and through a clump of birches, only to find not a sign of anything except an unearthly silence that had replaced the usual continual bird song. Over the next knoll a rough path led to the river and eventually back to where I had started. So it must have been while I was winding my way through the waist high bracken and dwarf birches and willow that grew sparsely on that knoll that the peregrine must have flown off with her prize, for when I reached the path only a few grey feathers bore witness to a wood pigeon's demise.

Sightings of red kites in the area have increased considerably during the years since they have been re-introduced into the Highlands. The programme started in 1989 and in the next four years ninety-three young birds from Sweden were released under a joint initiative between the RSPB and the Government's UK conservation agency. Breeding first occurred in 1992 and since then many of the pairs have established territories and raised young. With the aid of tiny radio transmitters fitted to them their progress can be easily monitored. It has been found that although the birds wander quite long distances from their release site they tend to breed relatively close to it, which is very convenient for the researchers. One bird that I know of, who was released from somewhere on the Black Isle, was radio tracked to Orkney and eventually established a territory in Perthshire. Both my sightings of these striking birds on home territory were around the beginning of autumn. One was just flying over the garden and did not stay long but the other was quartering an area of rough sheep pasture, which bordered a conifer plantation. When I first saw it I thought it was a buzzard, but as it banked to retrace its steps the long wings held at an angle and the distinctive deeply forked tail was a give-away to its identification. I sat watching it for a full five minutes before it soared out of sight over the forestry plantation and into the Ross-shire wilderness. What makes these raptors so attractive is the very rich colour contrast of their plumage. The pale grey head merges into the reddish brown almost chestnut upper parts and the brilliant white underwing patches appear to flash a message as this magnificent bird twists and turns in its endless search for food. One of the countries where the red kite and its close relative the black kite can be found in large numbers is Spain, where their regal status appears somewhat tarnished as they squabble over scraps at the local rubbish tips.

The garden wildlife is not just restricted to birds as a variety of mammals, amphibians and butterflies find this relatively tranquil setting to their liking. Between February and March one of the small ponds is invaded by an army of common frogs and the croaks from the males as they pair up with the females can be quite loud considering their size. Then after spending days, sometimes weeks, locked together the spawn is laid suddenly in one batch usually in the morning. The jelly coating around the eggs swells in the water and a great mat is formed in two or three corners of the pond as spawn from dozens of females collect together. After spawning the frogs spend the rest of the year in amongst the damp places around the garden feeding on insects, slugs, snails and earthworms. Their smooth, moist skin in its usual livery of mottled shades of green, yellow and brown is complimented in the Highlands by more vivid and distinctive shades of red and orange. Another creature of the pond, bog and sphagnum moss is the palmate newt which is the smallest of our three native species and favours moorland and heathland that the common and rare great crested newt shun. In the late evening or early night rustling sounds can be heard under trees and shrubs as the common toads begin to move out of their daytime retreats to hunt for food. These muddy, brown, warty skinned amphibians are the gardeners' friends as they can devour hundreds of insect pests, slugs and snails in a single nights foray.

Many of the resident small mammals are never seen until one of the cats deposit its dead prize on the dining room floor, which is not altogether appreciated. Field and wood mice, short-tailed voles and shrews have all found their way unwittingly into the house, many of them alive that have to be caught by yours truly and released back into the garden. Once I found one of the cats on the vegetable plot playing with a weasel it had just caught. This fierce little hunter, Britain's smallest carnivore, had to be treated with the utmost respect by cat and human alike, for his teeth penetrated a thick leather riggers glove to find a very vulnerable finger - some reward for his rescuer. The only time I have seen a stoat in the garden was on one early winters morning when I was breaking up some ice that had formed on the pond overnight to enable the ducks to bathe. Having been disturbed by the commotion this large male suddenly appeared from the direction of the incoming waterway, haired across the frozen pond with his black tipped tail trailing in his wake and disappeared over the perimeter stone wall, never to be seen again. This slim, lithe and most savage of predators mainly preys on rabbits which are more than twice its own size but I think it was abandoned duck eggs that this particular stoat was after.

One of the most exciting natural aspects of the actual house is its resident small bat population. Contrary to most people's views I love bats, but unfortunately like reptiles they are objects of irrational and superstitious fear. One such fear is that bats get entangled in women's hair but this is totally untrue as tests prove that bats cannot cling onto hair and just slip off. This fallacy probably derived from the seventeenth century when houses did not have ceilings and bats roosting in the rafters would sometimes fall down onto a woman below and become entangled in their hair nets. With a bats superb echo-location system that it uses for locating prey as small as gnats and for manoeuvring around at night the chance of becoming entangled in anything is highly unlikely. A small colony of pipistrelle bats live in the roof space of the old original house and can be seen fluttering over the pond with frequent twists and dives chasing small flying insects and moths as dusk falls on warm summer nights. One year I placed a bat box on a large silver birch tree that was growing amongst the dwarf birch and willow scrub on the other side of the watercourse. I inspected it after a couple of months to find to my surprise eight long-eared bats clinging to the inside of the box. The long-eared bats huge ears are part of an extremely sensitive echo-location system which being principally a woodland bat enables it to thread its way through the branches and dense foliage and also to distinguish between its prey and the leaf that it is on. Unlike other bats it feeds extensively on insects and larvae that it picks off leaves or bark whilst hovering on broad rounded wings. The structure of these wings also allows for a slow, fine, controlled flight for easy movement in small spaces. Bats are fascinating creatures that do not deserve their bad reputation for they are a truly remarkable animal being able to use their own intricate radar system, possess a skilful hibernation technique, sustain delayed fertilisation and are unique in being the only true flying mammal.

There are small numbers of two species of deer, which inhabit the surrounding woodland, the indigenous roe and the sika that is a native of eastern Asia but was introduced into Britain about one hundred and twenty years ago. The roe deer generally keep to cover and are usually only seen at dawn or dusk skipping across open spaces between dense thicket. One summer we had the company of a beautiful roe buck in the garden for a few days that advertised his presence by scent marking some of the trees in the small conifer copse. The scent gland, which is located on the centre of his forehead, was rubbed on the thin young pine trees where his hard and fully grown antlers stripped the bark off either side of the trunk, which could eventually kill the trees. Thankfully he soon moved on to pastures new to find a more suitable territory. Like the roe, sika stags and hinds can occasionally be seen grazing in the clearings throughout the adjoining woodland but my best views have been in the garden in the heart of winter when food is scarce. One stag in particular spent quite a considerable amount of time with us on several winters, judging by the amount of droppings deposited in the conifer copse, mainly eating any remaining nourishing grass and plants but also grazing a certain ornamental evergreen garden shrub. Not appreciated, but this was a small price to pay for the privilege of seeing this truly magnificent stag in prime condition, sporting a full set of antlers and pawing away a light covering of snow with his front hoof to reveal a hidden mouthful of sustenance.

One of the most colourful creatures of the garden in summer time are the butterflies. The most numerous is the small tortoiseshell, the most familiar of British butterflies, who live throughout the winter by hibernating in garden sheds, garages, barns and even enter houses to rest under pelmets and behind curtains. They emerge back into the garden in April to lay their eggs on nettle leaves, which lead to a generation of butterflies in July. These in turn lay eggs to produce butterflies in September and these are the ones that hibernate. With this extensive breeding cycle it is not surprising that the small tortoiseshell is seen almost everywhere in Britain including Shetland.

Other 'aristocrat' butterflies (a term devised by early entomologists for the largest and most colourful in the British countryside) that frequent the garden at variable times of the year are the beautiful red admiral and painted lady. Both these species being unable to survive a British winter migrate from the Continent or North Africa. These sparkling gems spend a lot of time feeding on the buddleia's we have planted and the scabious and clover that grow wild around the edges of the woods. We also have stinging nettle patches, which are the breeding grounds for 'aristocrat' butterflies although the adults do not feed on the drab flowers, as they are a poor source of nectar. More that forty species of insects including aphids, bugs and beetles are dependant on nettles for food and shelter. Other common butterflies in the garden include the meadow brown, small heath and common blue but the unusual ones are confined to the adjoining moorland. A clouded yellow, a regular but scarce migrant from southern Europe patrols the open areas in search of its food plant, the pea family that includes trefoils and clover. A small copper, uncommon in northern Scotland and the sole remaining member of the British coppers, basks on a heather flower and the Scotch argus, exclusively a Scottish butterfly, dances across the moors when the sun shines but immediately it goes behind a cloud disappears to rest in amongst the long grass and heather stems.

Away from the periphery of the house and garden grounds but lying within a radius of about half a mile are various habitats that have supplied us with a variety of wildlife encounters. To the north of the property, after negotiating our access track and passing through a small stand of Scots pines, a fenced area with a gated entrance is reached. This is an area known locally as 'the goat wife', where many years ago a woman from Dumfries (Aunt Dorothy) descended upon this small croft together with a multitude of animals including dogs, cats, 60 hens, 10 ducks and a flock of some 50 goats and kids and where a book of the same name was first published in 1939. The book, written by her nephew Alasdair Alpin MacGregor, is about her life at the croft (Cnocnamoine), the local people and the surrounding area that Aunt Dorothy enjoyed until her death on the 3rd May 1923. Unbelievably the croft house has remained uninhabited since that day and all that remains today are broken down walls and grass encrusted foundations of the porch and outhouses. Amazingly one gable end with chimney stack, which now serves as a jackdaw nest site, is all that is intact to indicate the height and size of the house. The area surrounding the house, that stands on a grass plateau, is covered by a small mature Scots pine plantation that was originally planted by Aunt Dorothy and her nephew but the individual specimens which are dotted around the heather moorland attract amongst other birds the rare Scottish crossbill. This was where I saw my first, a small flock of three brick-red males and accompanying yellow-green females stuffing pine seeds into their appropriate speckled olive-green young.

This was also where I came across one of the rarest mammals in Britain, the pine marten. My attention was first drawn to an open area of moorland where several jackdaws were dive-bombing what appeared to be a group of lichen covered boulders. Imagine my surprise when suddenly an animal the size of a large cat leapt onto the top of the boulders and lashed out at the annoying birds. I could not believe my eyes, a pine marten, who is rarely seen in daylight, standing there in full view with his striking creamy-yellow throat with matching inner ears, long rich brown fur and bushy tail. I had seen their tracks and droppings in the wooded area much further north but this elusive animal is very difficult to find. He suddenly realized he was not alone and shot behind a broken down stone wall which was draped in a rambling bramble bush and just disappeared. Just like his fellow mustelidae, the otter, now you see him now you don't. Mainly active at night these tenacious predators have been persecuted by game-keepers for years, which led to a serious decline, but fortunately new conifer plantations have enabled this very charismatic creature to increase. Being one of the most agile predators nothing is beyond his reach, from climbing trees in search of red squirrels, hatchling birds or eggs to swimming a loch to predate on island nesting birds like the black throated diver.

Another of the mustelidaes was a further source of amusement on another visit to Aunt Dorothy's. A stones throw from what remained of the house was a stone wall that encompassed a large sycamore tree, which during the autumn scattered its helicopter seeds far and wide. This dilapidated wall provided a play area for a family of stoats. This fiercest of predators, whose main prey is rabbits that are indeed twice its size, turns into a sweet and enduring creature when otherwise engaged. This was indeed so when five young and their mother decided to play tag amongst the loose stones that made up the wall. My first impression was an army of stoats scurrying around between the rock crevices, in and out, up and down, with their little black tail tips acting like beacons. They were so fast that sometimes they were just a blur. It is said that in northern Scotland stoats turn white in winter when they are then called ermine, but in my part of the Highlands I have only seen them go partially white which gives them a patchy appearance but always with the highly visible black tip to their tail.

To the west of the sycamore stood an isolated rendered wall at the head of what remained of an orchard. This wall was all that was left of Aunt Dorothy's hot-houses and along with a very productive plum tree was the only survivor of a previously well tended garden. Beyond the wall were the remnants of the Scots pines originally planted by her and beyond that the wide open moorland stretched towards Carn Bren. It was amongst the small plantation of old, twisted and broken pines that I encountered two of the most attractive birds of the woodland. The first was by sheer chance. As I was walking through the trees to the moors I suddenly heard what appeared to be baby birds chittering. It sounded quite close, but as all the pines had lost their lower branches (as they do) and the canopy was a good thirty feet high, I was baffled. I then realized the sounds were coming from a hole twelve feet from the ground, excavated in a long dead pine trunk that had lost most of its red scaly bark. A greater spotted woodpecker I thought. Knowing how territorial they are I hid behind another much larger trunk and proceeded to tap on the hollow wood mimicking the birds territorial drumming. Almost immediately came a reply and this was followed by one of the parent birds clamping onto the side of the nest hole. It was the male, with his red-nape patch glistening in the sunlight. After feeding the noisy young he took off to resume his duties.

The second bird, which sometimes nests in tree holes, appeared from nowhere. Perched on the lower hanging branches of one of the magnificent Scots pine specimens on the edge of the plantation was one of Britain's most colourful small birds. It was an adult male redstart with his rust-coloured tail, reddish belly, grey back, black throat and white forehead uttering an anxious "wee-ticc-ticc" alarm note, warning his family of my approach. This area of fragmented woodland is a sadder and less colourful place when these attractive breeding birds depart for tropical Africa in the autumn.

South of the 'goat-wife' the heather moorland rises then falls through sparse mixed woodland to the river below. The river that starts its life in the foothills of Carn Bren runs through several small waterfalls into the Kyle of Sutherland. It was just above one of these small but perfectly formed waterfalls that a colony of sand martins had their nests. Sited in a vertical sandbank formed by the continual erosion of the bank by wind, rain and river levels, the collapsed nesting tunnels are dug out by the adults after returning in the spring from equatorial West Africa. The horizontal tunnels can be three feet long with an enlarged area at the end to form a nest chamber. The smallest member of the 'hirundine' family can be clearly identified when in flight by a brown band across its distinctive white breast but characteristically no white rump like the house martin. When we first moved to the area there were only a few pairs but now there is a small but significant colony. There is something to be said for standing on a raised river-bed between two tributaries watching the unconcerned adult birds catching insects on the wing and disappearing into the nest holes to feed their young.

It was on this raised river-bed that one year we discovered a common sandpipers nest containing four buff and speckled chestnut brown eggs, lying in a sparsely lined scrape amongst the pebbles sheltered by a small alder bush. The adult bird was making quite a fuss and trying to distract us away from the nest site by pretending to be hurt and as she was showing signs of obvious distress we left immediately. On our return a few days later we discovered an empty nest containing several cracked eggs which could have been caused by predators or more likely the young could have hatched and left as soon as their down was dry. This rapid departure from the nest is common to most waders in order to reduce the risk of predation.

This attractive stretch of water is a typical mountain burn, fast flowing but not too deep, with a boulder strewn riverbed and small interspersed waterfalls that glisten in the morning sun acting as a magnet for two of our favourite upland birds. The plump, wren-like bird with the distinctive white breast – the dipper, and the elegant little grey and yellow bird with the long bobbing tail – the grey wagtail. Both species breed alongside the burn or next to the waterfalls and spend the spring and summer months complimenting this picturesque little burn which we affectionately call ours.

These are some of the many wildlife encounters we have experienced around our home and nature being what it is, there is always something new to see and learn around the corner - literally.

Chapter 2

LOCAL TERRITORY

RED SQUIRREL

From our sun lounge the land stretches away down to the narrow waters of the Inner Dornoch Firth before rising again on the north shore, which is covered by a large conifer plantation. Protruding majestically above and beyond this dark green carpet is Migdale Rock, a small but prominent granite hill with small areas of lime rich rock soil which has given rise to a diverse ground flora and sparse outcrops of fledgling Scots pine. Migdale Rock was formed by glacial ice flowing upstream that produced a smooth gently sloping side caused by abrasion, then flowing downstream, which tore away large pieces of rock to produce a rough, irregular and steep side. In geological terms this is known as "rockes moutonnées" and is very common in the west but rare in east Sutherland.

When we first arrived in Ardgay, Migdale Rock and the surrounding woodland, which was owned by Skibo Estate, was a tranquil place of beauty but before long the pine trees within the mixed woodland adjoining the loch were marked for valuation and possible felling. This would have totally devastated a very special habitat unique to the area for very little financial reward. After protests from local people and discussions with a Skibo Trust member it was revealed that the valuation was for tax purposes only, but the suspicions still remained until after a few more peaceful years the situation was finally resolved. The estate was originally owned by the late Andrew Carnegie and had since passed to his daughter Mrs. Margaret Carnegie-Miller. When Mrs. Miller died the governing estate trust decided that this part of the estate should be sold to a conservation body as a lasting memorial to the late Carnegie's and a long-term amenity to the local community. After being offered at a reduced price to several including the RSPB, it was eventually sold to the Woodland Trust whose origin was based in Lincolnshire but had just started making inroads into Scotland with a new branch office in Perthshire. So in 1993 the Trust purchased the then called Ledmore and Migdale woods, a truly magnificent 1756 acres site of variable habitats consisting of Scots pine, oak and birch woodland, heather moorland, valley bog, conifer plantations and rocky crags. This was by far the largest area ever acquired by the Trust. With financial contributions made by Scottish Natural Heritage and the National

Heritage Memorial Fund towards the purchase, this exceptional landscape and its wildlife was now safeguarded for generations to come.

The reserve contains three extensive SSSI's (Sites of Special Scientific Interest), the Ledmore oakwood, the Scots pinewood surrounding Migdale Rock and Spinningdale bog. The 235 acre Ledmore oakwood is the largest remnant of oakwood in Sutherland and the most northerly extensive oakwood in eastern Britain. The 355 acre Migdale pinewood, although probably planted many years ago by the estate, does exhibit characteristics of naturally occurring Caledonian pinewoods and again is one of the most northerly pinewoods in Britain. The 72 acre Spinningdale bog is the only example of a valley bog in east Sutherland, consisting of open water with reed beds leading to alder, birch and willow scrub. The loch, although not part of the purchase, does make an important contribution to the beauty of the reserve coupled with the diversity of the wildlife attracted to its tranquil waters. Although only three miles from the village of Bonar Bridge the reserve is quiet, peaceful and generally left to nature, apart from the occasional few walking along the loch side during weekends and bank holidays in the summer months.

There are two ways to approach the loch, one nearest the village where the public road ends at the loch side and the other which entails about a mile walk through mixed woodland starting from deep within the reserve. The advantage of the Bonar Bridge end is that the resident water birds can be observed without disturbance from a vehicle parked at the waters edge. In the spring the most numerous and noisiest are the black-headed gulls who breed on a small island at this end of the loch. Although very common in most parts of Britain, a colony of these gregarious gulls is quite rare for this part of the world. I know of only three others. Another of the residents is a pair of the very elegant mute swans who over the years have constructed an enormous mound of dead and decaying water plants as a nest site secreted amongst the dense reed bed, which is inaccessible from the road. I have often been the victim of the male's threat display where upon he draws back his neck, folds his huge wings above his back and surges forward in the water whilst delivering a loud aggressive hiss in defiant mood. Other wildfowl include mallard, tufted duck and during the winter months, goldeneye. The tufted duck has become a familiar sight on urban lakes, ponds and reservoirs and is now Britain's commonest diving duck. At a distance the male is just a black duck with snow white flanks but close up the head has a deep purple gloss crowned with a small long tuft that drops behind. In the winter the 'tuftie' is not only joined by small numbers of goldeneye but also by a few pochards. Although a close relative, the pochard has not yet colonised the vast areas of gravel pits and reservoirs created by man like the tufted. Like many species of duck the female's plumage is a dull brown, especially adopted for camouflage, but the males brick-red head, black breast and grey back is in contrast very distinctive. The goldeneye female is again very plain but the male is a real dandy. On the water he appears mainly white with a black head that has a green sheen, but what is most noticeable is the large white spot on each cheek. Another characteristic of the goldeneye is that when in flight both sexes have large white wing patches and their wings make a whistling sound. Normally the goldeneye is only a winter visitor that breeds in northern Scandinavia and northern Asia but since 1970 small numbers have bred in Speyside and are increasing using nest boxes which are attached to waterside trees, for goldeneye like the goosander prefer to nest in holes in hollow trees.

Being relatively close to the village and near to surrounding houses and the local fish farm, this end of the loch can appear somewhat overcrowded so I tend to approach the loch from a different locality. Instead of branching off I continue past a few small croft houses before rising onto the open moors then to descend abruptly through the mixed woodland within the reserve boundaries behind Migdale Rock where I park the Land Rover opposite a small grass covered track that eventually leads to the lochside. Like with most walkers through the countryside, some days you see hardly anything mentionable and others are so full of incidents as to appear untrue. There was such a day one late May. It was a bright clear morning and the sun had just begun to warm the atmosphere after a chilly night. We had acquired a dog the previous summer, a liver and white English Springer Spaniel bitch who was champing at the bit to get out of the vehicle. She is small, as springers go, with a very fluffy coat and long feathers on her legs, not a full tail but not a stump either, with a slight plume. Her most redeeming features are her big brown eyes and the different expression she has for every situation. Even as a puppy when we went to choose between eight bundles of fluff, the look she gave would have melted the hardest of hearts. From a very early age she responded more to the whistle than spoken commands, a legacy from her working strain parentage I suppose, although she has always been treated as a pet rather than a working dog. Like all springer spaniels her greatest asset is her nose. Her ability to find something interesting concealed within the undergrowth even fifty yards away is truly remarkable. This gift has been most helpful to me on many occasions when without her some of nature's secrets would have remained so.

Originally a pedestrian right of way the track had been widened and surfaced with stone chippings many years ago to allow vehicle access to extract thinnings from the small stand of Scots pine that was planted just before this end of the loch. Since that time recolonisation of plants, grasses and heathers had reverted the sterile gravel track back to its original condition of blending in with the natural environment. The surrounding natural woodland which stretched over much of the reserve consisted mainly of birch, interspersed with oak, willow, rowan and Scots pine with an under carpet of heather, bracken, bilberry and juniper - a dogs' and naturalists' paradise. Once off the lead Bracken (as I had called her for obvious reasons) began doing what springers do best, foraging through the undergrowth with her nose to the ground and tail waging continuously in total contentment. About thirty yards along the track a small clearing had been cut underneath the power lines that supplied the only two private houses within the reserve with electricity. These clearings, which had by now become sparsely covered by small birch, pine seedlings and willow scrub, were alive with movement and song. The ever present willow warblers were singing at the tops of their voices, one from an overhanging willow branch on one side and another from the very top of a small pine on the other side, clearly in competition but resolutely keeping to a designated chosen territory. Some regard the first swallow or cuckoo as a sign that spring has arrived but I always listen for the sweet descending call that heralds the willow warblers' return from far off southern Africa. This 'little brown job' is the most widely distributed of all the birds that are summer visitors to Britain and judging by the amount of calling during the breeding season most of them are in the Scottish Highlands. I was just about to continue when I noticed a small bird dart out from a small birch tree, catch a flying insect and return to the same perch. This was the unmistakable and usual behaviour of a spotted flycatcher and this must have been one of the first to arrive from its wintering quarters in central Africa. A rather nondescript grey and pale brown bird but with a bright and heavily streaked breast, that has a habit of sitting bolt upright when perched on a convenient branch or wire awaiting a passing insect.

A little further on two small shallow burns ran under the track and this was where Bracken's love of water could have ended in disaster. Having heard the water tumbling over the rocks and boulders she ran down the bank, splashed into the water and disappeared through the culvert that allowed the water to pass under the track. Although she performed this action many times on her walks when she was a puppy, only once did she nearly get stuck but panic always sets in on every occasion. Luckily after a few minutes she arrived at the other end none the worse for wear except for being slightly grubby and wet with an expression of 'what's up' written across her face. Her emergence had disturbed a pair of bullfinches, which quickly flew onto the next willow shrub, flashing their conspicuous white rumps as they went. These, one of Britain's prettiest birds, are nearly always seen in pairs with the males striking red underparts and black cap contrasting beautifully with the females same basic plumage but with salmon-pink underparts. The bullfinch and the spotted flycatcher are amazingly included on the 'Red List' which was compiled by well known bird conservation bodies using the data from national surveys to underline the rapidly declining population or range, recently or historically, and the global concern of certain species. These two along with other so called common species such as the skylark, song thrush, linnet and reed bunting qualify due to at least a 50% decline in the UK breeding numbers, or range, over the past twenty five years, a sad reflection on this country's common agricultural policy. Weed-free landscapes ultimately lead to no wildflowers and no insects, followed by a butterfly and bird-free countryside. This coupled with loss of land to roads and development puts further pressure on nature and the environment. Luckily the Highlands of Scotland have not succumbed to these problems and never will, as the very geology of the land will not allow these transitions.

The track continued through an avenue of birch and willow scrub before climbing through a more open aspect of specimen silver birch and Scots pine whose roots were covered by a dense growth of heather, bilberry and the ever-encroaching bracken. This was where early one autumn morning the silence was broken by the unnerving sound of a red deer stag roaring his defiance to any potential rivals within his territory. He was very close and as the mist began to slowly envelop the bracken covered knoll from where the roaring was apparently coming, I began to feel decidedly uneasy. Stags can be very unpredictable and dangerous at this time of year (the rut) as anything or anyone is regarded as a potential challenger to his supremacy. I began to look for a suitable tree to climb if the need arose but I needn't have worried because as we moved down-wind the eerie silence returned. The scent of man and his dog was too much even for the monarch of the glen.

Close to where I had stopped a lone hawthorn tree stood, clothed in a pastel green mantle of lichens. Stripped of its summer green leaves it looked positively ghost like with its bark absolutely covered in one of the commonest lichens -Hypogymnia Physodes, a glaucous grey coral shaped structure and the grey-green hanging tufts of Usnea subfloridana. Lichen plants are composed of a fungus growing in close association with an alga, which is usually a common form. Most lichens are highly sensitive to air pollution and particularly to levels of sulphur dioxide, so this grey skeleton in the mist spoke silent volumes concerning the cleanliness and freshness of the

Scottish Highland air.

But this was a totally different season where the bracken was just beginning to show its new green growth through the rust coloured hue of winter and the birches and willows were wearing their apple green foliage with pride. A metallic 'chak chak' quickly brought me to my senses; a black-headed male stonechat was announcing his presence from the top of a broken Scots pine branch that was sticking out from the heather. Although wonderful to see it wasn't the stonechat that was holding my attention, for in the far distance beyond the bird a female roe deer was ploughing through the bracken towards the stand of pines that cloaked the easterly slope of Migdale Rock. She kept stopping and looking back into the bracken behind her, which was odd. It wasn't until she hopped over a large boulder that protruded above the bracken that I realised why she had been so tentative, for following in her wake was a small new-born fawn. Having heard or sensed the dog she must have returned to lead the youngster from its hiding place amongst the vegetation to a safer spot. This adorable little creature had a sandy-brown coat flecked with black and white spots down the side and back, a real life "Bamby". These attractive spots will soon start to fade away and disappear totally when the fawn has grown its first winters' coat.

From here the track started to rise to its highest point far above the burn that meandered through the ravine into the bog and eventually tumbled into the Inner Dornoch Firth at Spinningdale. As we started to descend down to the loch Bracken suddenly stiffened, raised one paw like a pointer and sniffed the air. Something was around but I could not see or hear anything apart from a flock of siskins chittering in the nearby pines. Suddenly two sika hinds started to make their way through the brush on the other side of the burn. I called Bracken back as she started to bound through the undergrowth in their direction, amazingly she returned immediately and sat beside my legs watching them disappear in a tangle of trees - growing up already I thought.

About thirty yards further on the track forked into two, one dropping down over a concrete bridge to emerge at a pebble beach fringing the southern end of the loch and the other skirting the eastern shoreline. This clearing was where I had seen my first Scottish crossbills many years ago. What had first aroused my interest was the sound of pine cones falling to the ground. This was either a large family of squirrels or crossbills and as squirrels are rather thin on the ground in Sutherland I figured it must be the latter. Sure enough, high in two or three medium sized Scots pines was a flock of about eight birds; two bright red males, some apple green females and the rest were very speckled youngsters. Although quite rare in the area red squirrels do inhabit the reserve but mainly within the conifer plantation that is situated on the outskirts of Spinningdale village. The plantation is due to be thinned but with careful planning the colony should not be too disturbed. The red squirrel was one of the last mammals to colonise Britain before it was cut off from the rest of Europe and until the 1940's was fairly widespread. It has now disappeared from large areas of the country to be replaced by the grey squirrel, which is an introduced species and native to the hardwood forests of the eastern United States. The grey squirrel has not yet reached the Highlands and is mainly confined to the central belt of Scotland whereas the red squirrels' stronghold is in Speyside around Aviemore, spreading north to south east Sutherland. The delightful red squirrel is particularly attractive in summer with its bright chestnut fur, paler bushy tail and small ear tufts that are especially long in winter. They live to about three years old and are hunted on the ground by foxes and birds of prey, but in the trees they are predated by that equally agile carnivore, the pine marten.

Instead of continuing along the lochside I has decided to take a detour by clambering through the bracken and heather which partially covered the far side of the path, traverse the lower slopes of Migdale Rock using small deer tracks, before returning to the path further along the loch. As we started to climb the gradual incline Bracken suddenly sniffed the air and darted into a small area of birch scrub. This action was quickly followed by the sound of flapping wings as a woodcock rose into the air and twisted and turned through the trees to make its escape, followed by a very optimistic dog. She often flushes woodcock and the occasional pheasant from dense undergrowth on several of our walks. Woodcock's tend to sit tight until the last possible moment hoping that their superb camouflage will help them to avoid detection but springers are gifted with excellent noses and are bred with the intention to flush game for the gun, but in my case the birds live to 'flight' another day. Although it is a wader, the woodcock has deserted the open marshes and is more likely to be seen in damp woodland containing open clearings with a good growth of bracken and brambles. Woodcock's need soft ground in which to feed where they probe with their long bills for earthworms, insect larvae and centipedes. During one severe winter Bracken found several dead birds after an extremely cold spell (down to -24°c one night) where the ground remained as hard as concrete for several weeks.

We continued to follow the inconspicuous deer and fox tracks accompanied by continuous bird song with Bracken making the occasional foray into the undergrowth, but continually checking where I was as she always does when not sure of her bearings. One bird song in particular stood out from the rest, the unforgettable two-phased song of the wood warbler. When we first arrived in the Highlands in 1982 the wood warbler was an uncommon migrant, but numbers have regularly increased and the sparsely located woodlands have benefited from its presence. Wood warblers are usually very elusive as they forage high in the canopy often hidden by the green foliage, but in this particular woodland the low broken branches of the Scots pine make excellent perches from which to emit their colourful song. This handsome bird had yellowish-green upperparts with a bold yellow eyestripe but the bright sulphur-yellow breast and throat was most noticeable when its head was thrown back to emit the trilling song. The first phase of the song was a series of single notes, which accelerate into a trill, and was repeated regularly. Interspersed was the second phase which consisted of a series of plaintive 'pew-pew-pew' notes growing gradually fainter, a bit like the descending notes of a tree pipit. Bracken was very good and just stood and waited while I watched the bird flit from one tree to another rendering his song from each branch in turn. Unlike most dogs of her age that would tear around disturbing everything in sight she would stay close while I studied the birds but she became very inquisitive when the subject was within nose reach.

Having had my fill of wood warbler I carried on negotiating my way through the ground litter of fallen branches and moss covered boulders that long ago had torn themselves from the craggy rock above. Bracken, who had raced on ahead, suddenly started to dig frantically next to an old rotting tree trunk which was lying half imbedded in the rich soft brown soil. When I eventually arrived she had already uncovered one large plain white egg and was busily excavating another. Judging by the size they once belonged to a very large bird and the discoloration indicated that they had been underground for some time. Having taken time to think about it and thumbed through the pages of my birds egg book, I came to the conclusion that they were probably greylag goose eggs. A few geese do inhabit the loch and have obviously started to breed. Considering they were deeply buried and next to a well trodden animal path I also came to the conclusion that it was possibly a fox's food cache from the previous winter that had either not been needed or not re-found. I decided to take them with me as in that condition they were no use to anybody and Bracken would only dig them up again the next time we passed by the spot.

Having replaced all the dug soil and covered it with a large stone to foil you know who, I called her away and began the slow descent to the loch side, passing an old dead birch tree that long ago had lost its crown and stood like a stone pillar from ancient Greece. Even the razor-strop fungus that had etched its way into the knarled bark was grey in death and as hard as concrete. As its common name suggests the fungus was once used for stropping or sharpening razors and also to make corn plasters, corks and used as tinder for kindling fires. The razor-strop (Piptoforus Betulinus) is a common non-edible bracket fungus that grows exclusively on birch trees and very mature ones can grow to enormous proportions. Approaching the main path, the slope gave way to a more level area where natural drainage from the hill had produced a slightly wetter boggy patch that had become covered in sphagnum moss bedecked by small clumps of beautiful yellow primroses. In southern areas of the British Isles the primrose starts to bloom in March heralding the arrival of spring and warmer days, but here in the north everything is about a month behind and they can be found in bloom right through May and June.

From here the path descends to the waters edge to run parallel to the loch before rising slightly to a small promontory which I had christened "the windy corner", as the wind seemed to whistle through the trees no matter what direction it appeared to be coming from. The evidence was all around as the many fallen and rotting tree trunks and stumps bear witness. Bracken liked to swim here where the small bay on the leeward side was much calmer. She raced down the well-trodden path before plunging into the water and stood there up to her belly waiting for me to throw her a stick to retrieve. She swam towards the stick, picked it up in her formidable teeth and headed for the shore. Once on dry land she shook vigorously, dropped the stick instantly and started to sniff the air. She then headed for a large stone that was imbedded in the gravel shore with water lapping around its base on the very point of the exposed corner. She was smelling a black, tarry, slimy substance that had been deposited on the top of the rock before we arrived. After pulling her away I had to tie her to a convenient tree to stop her 'eating' the evidence. I had seen droppings like this before but much larger on the West Highland coast and they belonged to the otter. Although not a pleasant task the smell of faeces is a good method for identification of the depositor. This had a strong somewhat fishy smell, which only confirmed that it could either be otter or mink, although mink droppings do smell rather musky. Mink were introduced to Britain from North America in the late 1920's to be kept captive on fur farms but many escaped and since 1930 have spread over most of the country becoming steadily more numerous and still extending their range, but I did not think they had yet reached the reserve. These thoughts were later realised when the following late winter as Bracken and I were walking along the same area of path a loud splash occurred, followed by a trail of bubbles leading from a rock barely ten yards away out into the loch. The next sequence of events happened in seconds. As I was waiting for a diving duck like a goldeneye to appear further into the loch, two broad flat whiskered heads with pale chests suddenly appeared on top of the same rock. Easily recognisable as otters these two small creatures instantly turned, dived and disappeared, as only otters know how. Since that time the droppings on the rock at the windy corner have become larger and full of small bones with a fishier smell, indicating that these were young otters that were trying to establish a new territory. Let us hope that they succeed, as otters living on the reserve is indeed a bonus.

From the windy corner to the boundary of the reserve was a further one hundred yards or so along the track that was lined on each side by juniper bushes of various ages, most young, virile and green but a few old and virtually bear. The juniper is one of Britain's native conifers and the specimen bushes or small trees had spiky blue-green needles adorned with fresh green berries and a few surviving dark purple ones which had ripened in their second or third year. This small copse of mainly birch, rowan, aspen, oak and the odd Scots pine acts as a catchment area for many of the reserves songbirds including willow warbler, all of the tit family, robin, wren, blackbird and the vastly diminishing redstart. Redstart numbers have gradually decreased since I moved to the Highlands but on one occasion in this copse I was lucky to see the flashing orange tail of the otherwise dull brown female as she fed her four youngsters and the brightly coloured male as he stood guard close by.

Having reached the boundary sign Bracken and I turned back to retrace our steps. As we did so the "kwuk-kwuk-kwuk" flight call of a red-throated diver pierced the air as it flew down the loch before splashing down at the furthest and widest part which unfortunately was miles away from me - typical. These spectacular birds only visit Loch Migdale to feed on the bountiful supply of small fish but prefer the much smaller local hill lochans on which to breed. It is a real treat to be able to see these super birds on a regular basis with their deep red throats gleaming in the sunlight when caught at the right angle.

There are many dead and dying trees on this part of the reserve either from old age, disease or having been blown over. The fallers have decayed back into the ground and play host to fungi, lichens and mosses but others are just about standing even though peppered with insects and nest holes. It was in one of these dead but not quite rotten trees that our last unusual encounter occurred as we made our way back. Amid all the bird song around us a familiar "tchick-tchick" rang through the trees from the direction of the loch. Bracken raised her front paw as she always did when an unfamiliar sound or sight disturbed her, but I knew what it was and crouched down immediately trying to blend in with the surroundings. Unfortunately being liver and white Bracken was somewhat conspicuous but quickly ran to me wondering what I was doing. Holding her firmly and talking to her quietly to re-assure her I waited for the owner of the call to arrive. Sure enough, the undulating flight of the greater spotted woodpecker suddenly appeared through the trees, crossed the path and the black and white moth-like bird alighted onto a nearby tree. A quick look around, a short flight to a Scots pine stripped of its bark, before clinging on and adjacent to, a neatly chiselled hole in the trunk. Instantly a head popped out and was fed. The distinctive red nape patch of the male bird was obvious as he clung to the smooth trunk with his long clawed toes and balanced himself by bracing his fanned tail feathers. He quickly flew off before returning once again to feed the incubating female with small grubs he had found lurking behind some rotting tree bark. Earlier in the year the woods echoed to the characteristic drumming sound made by rapid blows of the bill on a dead bough as both sexes proclaimed ownership of the respective territory. This is now a fairly common sound throughout the mixed woodlands of south-east Sutherland and it is refreshing to know that the only species of woodpecker to inhabit the Scottish Highlands is flourishing.

The rest of the return journey was uneventful apart from being escorted from the reserve by the resident male buzzard. He sailed over the neighbouring hillside circling in the up draught from the hill, uttering his mewing "kiew-kiew", a now familiar sound in much of rural Britain. I have often said I could never again live where I could not see or hear the sound of soaring buzzards, to me the epitome of the wild, hilly country that I love and the guardians of the reserve.

Chapter 3

WINTER MAGIC

ROE DEER - (BUCK)

The day dawned with the type of December day in the Highlands that man and beast both relish. Bright blue sky, white fluffy clouds and despite a keen wind blowing from the south east, relatively mild for this time of year.

Feeling that I needed a day out to chase away the winter blues, I duly packed my rucksack with a flask, egg mayonnaise sandwiches and a piece of home-made chocolate cake. I certainly know how to live!

I had decided to walk up my favourite glen, which starts at Glencalvie through to Alladale and the wild hills beyond, to see if I could get some reasonable photographs of red deer stags. In the winter these magnificent animals adorned with their hard antlers come down from the high hills to the lower slopes where some are fed with potatoes by estate workers. This enables them to withstand the harsh Highland winters and some may then become the quarry of the trophy hunters in the stalking season from July to October. This policy of shooting the best stags has backfired on some estates, where they now have too few mature stags for breeding purposes.

Boarding my trusty Land Rover armed with camera, telephoto lens, binoculars and telescope I headed for the hills. To reach the clearing where I leave the Land Rover involves ten miles of very pleasant driving adjacent to a fast flowing salmon river bordered by birch, willow and alder scrub. At this time of year with the leaf buds firmly closed against the icy chill, small flocks of birds consisting of redpolls, great tits and blue tits can be seen flitting from branch to branch in search of that elusive meal that is so hard to find.

Half way along the glen I parked the vehicle off the road and after a short walk through the birches arrived at a small but most picturesque waterfall. It consists of three small falls each cascading into its own deep pool which in turn flows into the main river system. Often the plump little dipper can be seen dancing from stone to stone occasionally disappearing into the white water in search of insect larvae or small fish which are its staple diet. But not today. In cold winters they may move further down stream, even to lochs and estuaries to find warmer waters.

I returned to the vehicle and continued my journey along the winding road with only the occasional cry from a circling buzzard for company, when I stopped to chat to one of the local gamekeepers. This one is in tune with nature and often keeps me up to date with the latest information concerning the local wildlife. If only more were that interested in conservation we would not have the poisonings and trappings of the so-called 'vermin' in the Highlands. With his weathered face, black bushy beard and portly figure, garbed in breeches and deerstalker, he looked as though he had just stepped out of a country magazine. "The pine martens have been causing trouble again", he said, "getting in amongst the pheasants, might have to live trap and release in another area". Most keepers would not be so tolerant but with a little bit of give and take we can all live amicably.

After having parked the Land Rover in the clearing opposite the bridge that straddles the River Carron, I thought I would take a quick look round to see what had passed this way recently. The tell-tale footprints of roe deer embossed in the muddy track leading into the dark depths of the man-made forest and a fox dropping strategically placed on top of a grassy tussock to mark his territory. There is always something of interest if you know how to look, what to look for and what you are looking at.

Having hitched my rucksack onto my back, binoculars around my neck and telescope over my shoulder I began to walk along a stony track that eventually leads to an isolated hunting lodge nestling in the distant hills. The track follows the natural curvature of the river, which flows thirty feet below in a ravine gouged out by the continual erosion of fast flowing water on a limestone bed. The banks of the river are lined mainly with birch occasionally interspersed with Scots pine, willow and rowan. This is a perfect habitat for many species of small birds such as warblers, finches and tits, but on this early December day the crowns of the trees were covered with moving flocks of fieldfares. These Scandinavian thrushes arrive in early winter to escape the harsh north European weather to feed on the harvest of succulent red berries of the rowan tree, then they migrate further south before the hard frosts descend upon our northern latitudes. They are attractive birds that appear to want to keep me company, staying just far enough in front for me to pick out their slate grey heads, chestnut backs and pale rumps as they flit through the trees chattering to each other. Further along the track three pairs of bullfinches decide to put in an appearance, the brightly coloured males adding a touch of glamour to the otherwise relatively dull colours of a winter's day.

On I walked keeping one eye on the hills that rise from the opposite bank to nearly eight hundred feet and the other on the multitude of small waterfalls that make this one of the most attractive rivers in the area.

As I was approaching a small wooden bridge that crosses a tributary of the main river the clouds began to take on a grey mantle thus reducing the light needed for good photography. It was then that I saw them, four stags, heads down, feeding amongst the trees, their winter coats giving them almost complete camouflage against the dead bracken. They raised their heads to inspect the intruder and before they moved quietly away mingling with the background I could make out that three were about five years old and one a mature royal. There was no point in stalking them for a better picture because I could not approach them from this direction and from the other, being upwind, they would smell my scent.

I decided to try my luck further on and continued along the track that by now has begun to climb quite noticeably through mixed woodland until it reached 'my viewpoint'. This is a jumble of giant boulders covered in moss and heather, which is an ideal place for scanning the huge vista that unfolds before you. The river at this point is about one hundred and fifty feet below, meandering through a birch lined glen down from the far off wild and untamed hills.

After checking the time I decided to carry on a bit further to the red deer calving grounds and return to the viewpoint for a late lunch. The shale-covered track descends rather quickly to the glen floor and gives a different perspective to the rugged fifteen hundred foot hill that towered above me. I had been studying a small flock of redpolls that had been dancing through the scattered birches when I glanced up to see a large brown bird soar through a gap between the hills close to the summit. Even without the binoculars it was the unmistakable shape of the golden eagle. This was the male bird, smaller than the female, with a wingspan of just over six feet, and with just a touch of pale markings on the under-wing indicating that this was an adult bird. He soared away down the glen hugging the skyline searching for a deer or sheep carcass that had not long died, for eagles, unlike foxes, do not like their meals 'high'. It's amazing how nearly every time you spot a raptor it's going away from you. But this time I'm in luck. He banked to the left with the agility of a fighter pilot and headed towards me. As he got nearer, the detail of his majestic form began to unfold. Suddenly he dived and levelled out just below the summit of the rugged hill. Although he was difficult to pick out against the similar coloured background, once found, the spectacle of observing this king of birds in all his glory made me feel privileged to be allowed to share his world. As if on command the sun peeked out from behind a cloud for a few seconds and reflected from his golden crown as he disappeared behind the adjoining hill.

I continued further down the glen and after spotting some red deer hinds through the telescope decided to turn back as the time was getting on. The days really are short at this time of year. I had not gone a hundred yards when a brown bird of prey that I instantly mistook for a buzzard flapped slowly across my path. On further inspection the easily recognisable white rump was visible as she glided down towards the river. This female hen harrier would normally spend the winter hunting the marshes and sand dunes along the coastal fringe, but perhaps the mild winters that we have had in the north recently had enabled her to stay longer in her home territory, much to my delight.

As she continued to quarter the lower slopes of the rugged hill I continued to ascend to my viewpoint for a long awaited lunch. I had just taken a bite of my sandwich when a piercing scream echoed through the glen. I looked up to see the hen harrier alight from the heather below me with a mammal of some kind in her talons. This view of her was indeed special, as you do not often see a raptor observed from above. Although predominantly brown, apart from a white rump, the subtle markings of the feathers that knit together to form her wings were a revelation when viewed from this angle. Just as I was engrossed in watching her she disappeared behind a grassy knoll and my attention was quickly diverted to a rustling noise that came from my left. Three female sika deer suddenly emerged from some birch scrub on the opposite river bank, obviously disturbed by the harriers' antics, displaying their conspicuous white rumps which they flare to act as warming signals when alarmed. They continued to glance back at intervals as they too disappeared into the heather and bracken covered surroundings. This species is not native to Britain, but was introduced to a number of deer parks over 100 years ago. Wild herds in this area are derived from released animals that will sometimes interbreed with the red deer to produce hybrids.

All this activity happened so quickly that I had forgotten to take any photographs. I then finished my lunch to the accompaniment of the sound of the river below, interspersed by a robin proclaiming his territory from a distant vantage point.

My descent to the river level was uneventful until, as I approached the small wooden bridge, to my amazement, standing on the other side of the river-bank looking straight at me was the royal stag. He had been caught unawares by my presence and I by his. We just stood there transfixed, each wondering what the other would do. He was magnificent, his nose twitching for the merest scent, ears pricked forward and eyes staring, unblinking, in total concentration. His head was crowned with a fine set of hard antlers, the twelve points slightly peat stained from thrashing about during the rutting season. The muscles on his shoulders and flanks stood out like a well-trained athlete and were covered by his dark brown thick winter coat. Considering the time of year, when most stags are on the decline, he was in marvellous condition and a fine specimen.

I removed my rucksack from my back very carefully trying not to make any sudden movements and having taken out my camera, which was already fitted the telephoto lens, raised the viewfinder to my eye and there he was – gone. I looked up only to see his rump disappearing into the undergrowth. The sight of a long lens pointing at him, reminiscent of a gun, was too much to bear, for he had seen what had befallen some of his friends faced with the same situation. Who can blame him for taking to his heels, for man is the most dangerous animal on earth and all other species know it.

Obviously not a very successful photographic excursion but as I made my way back along the twisting track I could reflect on my good fortune at being able to spend a day exploring this truly beautiful untamed terrain in the company of rare wild creatures.

Chapter 4

WHERE EAGLES FLY

GOLDEN EAGLE

There are two National Nature Reserves within close proximity to each other situated in the north-west Highlands - Inverpolly in Wester Ross and Inchnadamph in Sutherland. Although both wild, rugged mountainous areas, they differ entirely regarding the habitats within their boundaries.

Inverpolly, covering an area of 26,827 acres is the second largest N.N.R. in Britain and contains a wealth of diverse landscapes consisting of seashore, marine islands, barren mountain tops and a scattering of birch, hazel and rowan woodlands. In contrast Inchnadamph occupies only 3,200 acres and consists mainly of a high limestone plateau with unique botanical and geological interest surrounded by high mountains.

It was a pleasant warm early June day with a slight south-westerly breeze blowing which would help to keep the midges at bay. Inchnadamph is especially well known for its rich and varied flora and at this time of year the very special 'mountain avens' would be in full flower. The full beauty of this rare plant lasts for only a few weeks and to catch it on film I would have to make tracks north-westwards.

The reserve is situated in the district known as Assynt, a wild, rugged and some would say desolate area of rock, mountains, lochans and very few trees. It lies between Loch Assynt and Sutherland's highest mountain, Ben More Assynt at 3,244 feet and has been a N.N.R. since 1956 under an agreement with the owner of Assynt Estates. The southern boundary of the reserve is the Allt nan Uamh burn that begins its journey from the slopes of Breabag (2,323 feet) joining the River Loanan before flowing into Loch Assynt. Excavations of caves found high above the burn have revealed bones of brown bear, arctic fox, reindeer, lynx and lemming which inhabited this part of Scotland around the time of the last Ice Age. Also found was evidence of occupation by Stone Age people, this being one of the earliest records of man inhabiting the Highlands.

The Stronchrubie cliffs mark the western limit of the reserve and are a great introduction to begin the exploration of one of the most interesting nature reserves in the entire country. The 300 ft. limestone cliffs, which line the main A837 road, have many ledges and crevices, which are ideal for buzzards, kestrels, hooded crows and many other cliff nesters to breed. Earlier in the year I had visited this area and discovered a pair of ravens with a healthy brood of three youngsters nesting on a crag surrounded by rowan and birch seedlings. When one of the parents arrived in the area of the nest site, the large black bird first proceeded to perch on an adjoining rock to make sure the coast was clear before flying in to feed its hungry brood. They raise only one brood each year, starting as early as February or March and this enables the large abandoned nest of sticks and heather stalks to be, as in this case, used by a pair of kestrels later in the year. The raven is a much maligned bird, perhaps because they were once common scavengers in the streets of London, but after years of persecution by man they have been driven into the more remote areas of Britain. Ravens, like the peregrines, are superb flying machines and their aerobatic courtship display is a delight to watch. I must admit to having a soft spot for the raven for many years. In this particular area I have experienced three of them flying in formation on escort duty along side my moving vehicle, red gaped youngsters being fed by the roadside and when walking in the hills having seen nothing exciting all day, you can bet a big, black bird with a diamond shaped tail will 'cronk' into sight to save the day.

Just past the cliffs next to the Inchnadamph Hotel a car park has been constructed for visitors to the reserve. After changing into walking boots and with my rucksack on my back containing the all important camera, I headed for the hills. After a short walk along the side of the road I was accompanied by the call of the elusive snipe somewhere in among the adjoining marshland and the more conspicuous lapwing displaying overhead. The walk begins after crossing over the bridge spanning the River Traligill. From here the track passes the old semi-derelict lodge, through the grounds and on to the hill ground grazed by sheep, cattle and the occasional Highland deer pony. It was here, sitting on the adjoining deer fence and bathing in a puddle formed by a depression in the track surface that was continually filled by the high rainfall in this area, that I saw my very first twite. Sometimes referred to as the 'mountain linnet' this bird's nondescript streaky brown plumage is no match for the chestnut back with red forehead and breast of its lowland counterpart. But in flight and courtship display the male twite shows his unusual shocking pink rump, which makes them about equal. Twite breed on heather covered moorland, rough hill pasture and bracken-clad hill country, particularly in the western Highlands and Ireland. In winter they desert the inhospitable high ground and form flocks with other finches feeding on seeds and insects in coastal areas.

The rough vehicle track winds its way up and up over a man made concrete ford bridging a hill burn, to end up at a picturesque holiday cottage nestling in the hillside some five hundred feet above sea level. A small waterfall can be seen from the ford where dippers bob up and down on exposed rocks and grey wagtails dance above the glistening water, catching insects in mid-air. Both sides of the track to the cottage are carpeted with heath spotted orchids in a variety of colours, from purple to pale pink through to white, poking their heads above the old heather stems. In small well-spaced patches the white tufts of cotton grass sway gently in the breeze adding further sparkle to the damp, boggy ground in which they thrive. Despite their name they are in fact sedges and the ball of cotton wool is fine hairs that surround each ovary when the flower head is ripe.

The small drainage ditches that run along the side of the track are encrusted with the two insectivorous plants that inhabit boggy moorland and damp heaths. The bright yellow-green star shaped curled leaves of the butterwort are a death trap to insects that become stuck on the sticky upper surfaces. The leaf instantly curls up engulfing the victim and secretes digestive enzymes that break down the insects' body extracting nitrates and phosphates that are lacking in acid moorland soils. In contrast to its character this plant has delicate violet flowers borne on long leafless stems which give rise to its other name of bog violet.

The sundew is the other plant that feeds on insects which again uses its leaf that is covered in a multitude of red hairs, each tipped with a glistening droplet, as a lure and trap. The insects are attracted to the droplets and once they touch the sticky fluid are held fast while the leaf margins curl inwards to entrap them. As before the plant secretes juices to break down the body to extract salts, which are absorbed through the leaf. The sundew is a much smaller plant than is perceived from photographs or television and this is borne out by the fact that its most common prey is the midge that it devours at the rate of 2000 in a single summer. At last a prolific destroyer of the dreaded Highland midge!

From the cottage the track reverts to a grass covered path although the steep incline of the initial thirty yards through the wooden gate is scarred by deep ruts, caused by four wheel drive vehicles used to transport deer carcasses and stalkers to and from the hills during the stalking season. The view from the top looking back from whence I came is breathtaking. The small white painted cottage in the foreground is dwarfed by the backdrop of the water of Loch Assynt stretching to the distant horizon flanked by the mass of Quinag. Suddenly the 'cronk, crock' of a raven broke the spell and I spun round to investigate. There in the sky about 100 yards in front of me flying across the small glen was the raven, following at a distance a much larger and totally silent bird. The distinctive size, shape and wing pattern of the other bird was unmistakable, the awesome figure of an adult golden eagle. The raven was obviously seeing the eagle off its territory albeit somewhat cautiously. As they approached the 2500 ft. western flank of Beinn an Thurain a further two eagles appeared from behind the ridge like World War II pilots being scrambled to combat the enemy. The smaller male engaged the intruder, as the raven realizing that discretion was the better part of valour, disappeared behind a grassy knowl. The resident male then buzzed the incomer a couple of times who then proceeded to about turn and return from whence it came, followed by the emerging raven cronking once again in defiance. The golden eagle is not strictly territorial and although it may drive off another eagle which ventures too near its nesting area (as in this case) it will not actively defend the area in which it lives. The hunting grounds of different pairs of eagles often overlap and they will even tolerate and indeed share the area with an immature bird or unmated adult. Having dealt with the threat to his domain the victorious male returned to his female. They appeared to greet each other and then proceeded to soar just above my head to advertise their continued residency. I in fact, was now lying on my back peering through my binoculars at this momentous spectacle. One eagle was so low that I could easily distinguish the streaked golden crown, massive hooked beak and that large, piercing hazel coloured eye that enables the eagle's visual acuity to be eight times greater than ours. I had never experienced eagles flying as close as this before and having a choice of which bird to focus on was an unusual luxury. They continued to circle above me for several minutes enabling a detailed scrutiny of this majestic bird. As if saying 'you have seen enough now, were off', the two birds although continuing to soar, moved slowly further and further away towards Quinag, eventually becoming two small specs in the distance.

After this encounter anything else was going to seem pretty trivial I thought as I made my way past the old sheep byre and a small stand of conifers planted many years ago as some sort of botanical experiment. Even these weather beaten and stunted conifers have their uses as they are home to a few pairs of siskin, redpoll, coal tits and even song thrushes who feed on the abundance of slugs and snails in the area.

Approaching the River Traligill the surrounding rough grassland and heather was alive with meadow pipits, joined by a few pairs of wheatears dancing from boulder to boulder flashing their white rumps to advertise their presence. This stretch of the river is only about twelve foot wide and crossed by a roughly constructed small wooden bridge. My jewel in this crown lay all around. Dotted along the far bank between the bridge and the tiny waterfall situated about 100 yards downstream were the creamy-white flowers of the mountain avens. This native evergreen shrub was clinging to the shallow soil that had infiltrated the many rock crevices caused by erosion of the soft limestone. The Latin name of 'Dryas Octopetala' comes from the name Dryad, the wood nymph of oaks, as the leaves are thought to resemble oak leaves. These plants are very rare except in north-west Scotland and the Burren on the west coast of Ireland.

Covering much of the mountain grassland were two species of lady's mantle. This is not one plant but a name afforded to several species, which vary in size and beauty. The two found in this area are the large leaved mountain variety of the more common lowland species and the smaller creeping alpine version. The leaves of alpine lady's mantle, which rise from the roots, are deeply divided into five to seven lobes, green above and silver below with pale green clustered flowers. It is a common plant in northern Scotland and Cumberland, but absent elsewhere.

As I was trying to capture the beauty of these rare mountain plants on film, I was distracted by the rapidly beating wings of a small dark bird flying directly down the course of the river towards the waterfall. Having completed my task I decided to investigate. At first I couldn't see the bird but then it suddenly appeared from under a rocky overhang and flew back up the river. This was the usual behaviour of a breeding dipper and there must be a nest close-by as it was obviously feeding young. I decided to settle down next to the waterfall and await its return. The dipper was nesting somewhere under the overhang of a large but shallow cave, formed by the constant battle between the very acidic waters of the river when in spate and the soft limestone of the underlying rock. This situation was further outlined by the disappearance of the river at the base of the cave, which followed an underground course to re-appear about a mile further downstream. Because of this geological phenomenon there are many signs of dried up riverbeds scarring this high plateau.

The waterfall, although small, sparkled like a precious gem as the sun peeked from behind a white fluffy cloud. The cool clear water gently roared as it dropped in two steps to the boulder-strewn base of the cave and disappeared into the dark depths of the underground caverns. The rocky sides of the waterfall were adorned with small clumps of mountain avens, alpine lady's mantle and yellow biting stonecrop with the occasional early purple flowering orchid, although past its best, adding colour to the surrounding grassy areas. Suddenly the dipper arrived back, perched on a rock at the base of the waterfall to make sure the coast was clear, then flew up to the nest, fed its offspring, then back down the river again. I was about to inspect the nest when a movement on the rock face caught my eye. Ferreting in and out of the crevices was a stoat. The rock face above the cave was about thirty foot high, covered in nooks and crannies with small stunted birch, rowan and willow scrub clinging to a spartan existence. The stoat, totally oblivious to me, was hunting for voles, shrews, fledglings or anything else he could find amongst the vegetation, as stoats are totally omnivorous. I feared for the dipper's young but the stoat obviously realised he could not reach the nest in that position and after investigating every accessible part of the rock face disappeared into the adjoining undergrowth, not to be seen again.

I climbed down to the waters edge and carefully picked my way over the protruding stones until I was in a position to inspect the nest. It was bulky and dome shaped, built mainly of moss, sitting precariously on a small ledge on an otherwise sheer rock face, hence stoat proof. It was lined with dead leaves and contained four youngsters of a few days old. Possibly the pair's second brood. I returned to my observation point just in time to see one of the parents alight onto the same boulder as before, but this time after feeding the young it returned to perch on the boulder for a preen and a rest. This plump wren-like bird with a white throat and breast gleaming in the sun was constantly bobbing and its white eyelids were blinking in unison. Just a little further downstream a pair of grey wagtails were walking along the waters edge, their tails constantly twitching up and down, watching for any unsuspecting insects. What a magical place this was.

After having torn myself away from the falls I retraced my steps back to the foot-bridge. From here the path leaves the river behind and crosses the plateau to end at the Traligill limestone caves that appear as black holes sunk into the distant hillside. Standing at the mouth of Gleann Dubh (a dark narrow valley) your eyes are first drawn to the shallow river as it meanders its way from the high tops, down the bealach between Beinn an Thurain and Conival, eventually to flow into Loch Assynt. Then to Conival itself, standing majestic on a bed of lewisian gneiss with her shattered quartzite cap glistening in the sunlight.

It is from here in the autumn that the sight and sounds of the rutting season of the red deer can be spectacularly observed. The courting and mating time lasts for about three weeks beginning in September and the hills echo to the stags bellowing roars. During the rest of the year the stags live quiet, unobtrusive lives in bachelor herds, building up their fat reserves on the rich summer grazing. Approaching the rut, they split up seeking out hinds to gather into a harem. Their success depends on age, size and how impressive they look and sound to other stags. Rival stags first try to out-roar each other, failing that they will walk side by side trying to assess each others strength. Evenly matched stags will sometimes fight, locking antlers as each tries to push the other backwards but fights to the death are rare.

One October I can remember seeing four mature stags, each with a harem of about eight hinds, patrolling their territory on the lower slopes of Beinn an Thurain. They were all roaring at intervals but none of them imposed on the others patch. Diplomacy at its height! Then suddenly a much louder, deeper roar came from a hidden valley and this intimidating sound appeared to disturb the other stags. After a few minutes of incessant roaring the culprit revealed himself followed by at least twenty grazing hinds. He was a magnificent beast of about eight years old and in prime condition with fully-grown antlers, thick neck and heavy mane. He was what is termed a royal stag, which have twelve points to their antlers and are much prized. The other stags who were slightly younger appeared to respect his authority as they slowly moved away to a safer distance, gathering their hinds as they went. But he was content and just stood on a rocky pinnacle bellowing his warning, a true monarch of the glen.

The path from here, although boggy in places, is well defined as it winds its way through the heather and rough grassland, which in turn is broken in places by scattered rocky outcrops. On approaching the caves or sinks, as they really are, the sound of rushing water is very apparent which is in total contrast to the quiet and peaceful glen. An underground river has eroded the limestone creating two adjoining sinks which both have steep rocky sides decorated with mountain avens, lady's mantle, primroses and assorted ferns. A miniature rock garden in an otherwise sparse landscape. The other cave is a true cave from where once the river tumbled before changing course. It is also the only available overhead cover in the immediate vicinity, although when it does rain, due to the porous rock, it's like standing in a shower. A most unusual feature of this cave, but a welcome surprise at the right time of year, is a small area of wild strawberry plants clinging to the shallow soil. The fruits are small but have a delicious flavour.

The noise from the water rushing through the underground caverns obscured any bird song, so I moved further up the knoll and sat in a small grassy depression surrounded by heather. Almost instantly I was rewarded, the 'chippa-chippa-chippa' call of a snipe broke the silence. Recognising the call is one thing, finding the bird is another. In my experience the snipe is a most elusive bird (other than when displaying) with his plumage blending in perfectly with the surroundings and in this terrain with the call bouncing off the enveloping hills, it makes this bird virtually impossible to find. Returning to my camouflaged position, I was aroused by distant piping 'pee-u, pee-u, pee-u' echoing through the glen. The call continued getting closer and closer each time until I was sure it was within range. From my high vantage position I scoured the low ground, paying particular attention to the many rocky outcrops, for if I was right this particular bird would be singing from his favourite song-post. Then I spotted him, perched on top of a far off lichen covered rock uttering his very clear contact call. Before I could focus my telescope on him he flew off, circled, then landed on a grass patch just below me and began searching for insects, earthworms or snails, which is his staple summer diet. Lying prostrate on the short heather and resting my telescope on a small boulder, I had my best view to date of the shy, nervous, mountain blackbird - the ring ouzel.

This adult male had a sooty-black plumage, white crescent on his breast and I could even see the pale edges to his flight feathers. He continued to search the surrounding vegetation for food until after a few minutes he appeared to become disturbed and agitated. The reason for his concern was apparent when the female suddenly arrived with a beak full of insects and showed considerable annoyance at his lack of success. She had a browny-grey plumage compared to the male and her breast crescent was less clearly marked. My luck then began to run out. After flying to the top of an adjacent hill, they spotted me and disappeared behind a small crag which overlooked the river, giving a harsh 'tac-tac-tac' call in alarm. From my previous rather scant sightings of this particular pair, it would appear that the nest site was located either in one of the numerous small trees that lined the river course or in a sheltered spot amongst the adjoining rocks or crags. Perhaps I will find it one day!

The ring ouzel, unlike its close relative the garden blackbird, is a summer visitor to upland Britain and winters mainly in the Atlas Mountains and around the Mediterranean. Although the two species look similar they have quite different characters. Blackbirds are tame, familiar birds of rural areas, whereas ring ouzels are shy, difficult to approach and rarely nest below 1,000 feet. They often have two broods further south, but in these northern latitudes one brood is the norm. I have often seen the juveniles, who lack the white crescent and resemble young blackbirds but are more heavily barred, sitting in the late summer sun on the stone walls that dissect the lower slopes of the glen, apparently contemplating their impending journey south.

On my return I stopped at the foot-bridge to take a drink from the cool mountain burn and reflect on my day. Many look at these wild, mountainous areas and think what a deserted, desolate place. But provided you use your eyes and ears, mother nature will provide a feast to set before a king.

Chapter 5

THE MAIDEN'S TRESSES

With spring creeping into summer the time had come to journey to the highest waterfall in Britain before the tourist season began. Eas Coul Aulin is officially 658 feet high (200m) which is four times higher that Niagara Falls but obviously not as wide and hides amongst the wild mountains of Assynt. Difficult to see from above it drops about 500 feet in three defined leaps followed by a white water tail of 150 feet or more.

There are three ways to reach the falls, an arduous walk of about eight miles from Inchnadamph, a lot shorter but rougher upland walk over a high saddle from Loch na Gainmhich or the easiest by boat from Kylesku to the head of Loch Glencoul. Being of more mature years I decided to opt for the softer option for a change and this decision had encouraged my wife to join me.

I had telephoned ahead on boat departure time and more importantly whether I could take my dog Bracken with me because I did not want to leave her in my vehicle for hours on end. My only concern was her over friendliness with the other passengers and being a springer spaniel her fondness for water.

My wife and I had left home around mid-morning for the leisurely drive to Kylesku, had lunch overlooking Loch Assynt before arriving at the tiny hamlet in plenty of time for the 14.00 hours sailing. We parked in the small car park, bought our tickets and walked down to the slipway to await the boats arrival. The slipway was the original used by the ferry that had been superseded by the Kylesku Bridge now towering above the narrows. The bridge, which has been used in many a car advert, initially stuck out like a sore-thumb but now it has weathered and with the grey concrete having lost its freshness, it now blends in with the three thousand million year old Lewisian Gneiss which forms the base of the surrounding hills.

Bracken was fascinated by the movement beneath the clear water adjacent to the slipway. Shore crabs scurried around in and out of the kelp and brown seaweeds scavenging for anything edible, small fish darted here and there, common starfish moved slowly over the rocky bottom in search of muscles and several umbrella-shaped common jellyfish swayed to and fro with the current. Strangely she didn't seem interested in going in for a swim, perhaps it was the depth of water straight from the side that bothered her as her normal entry into water is a gradual decline down a riverbank or from a beach. So this reaction dispelled my fears of her jumping into the loch from the boat that wouldn't have gone down too well with the other passengers.

As we stood on the slipway waiting for the boat to arrive from the previous trip further passengers arrived. People watching is a favourite pastime of mine and I was fascinated to see what type of people and how they were attired for the forthcoming boat trip. There was a multitude of guises, some were clad in walking boots and anoraks, as we were, but we had substituted walking boots for shoes, as the soles were softer for walking on the boat deck. Others were dressed in what I can only describe as town clothes and shoes accompanied by an umbrella. Some were old, some were young with children but none with dogs. We were a real motley crew but all hoping in anticipation to see something special.

Eventually the boat appeared as it chugged around the headland towards the jetty. Estimating the length of anything is not my forte but all I can say is that it appeared big enough to deal with any problems that might arise on a sea loch and accommodate the increasing number of passengers and still leave Bracken enough room to stretch her legs. Having waited for the boat to empty I hoisted my wife up onto the gunwale where she was closely followed by Bracken with me floundering in her wake. I positioned her between our legs as we sat down on one of the benches that lined the periphery of the deck. The boat continued to fill until all the passengers waiting on the quayside had been accommodated which still left plenty of room to breath. With the ropes slipped from their moorings the boat slowly moved into open water, came about and headed into the tranquil waters where the lochs of Glendhu and Glencoul join together.

From the direction in which the boat was travelling the plan was to sail down the right hand side to the head of the loch and then back down the left hand side to the quayside. Just as we entered the loch proper I noticed that there was a distinct line separating the green foliage clinging to the surrounding rock face from the bare almost barren upper reaches. Believe it or not, it appears that in the latest autumn gale the wind was so strong as it funnelled up the loch, it tore the vegetation (roots and all) from just above the water level at the time creating this bizarre scene.

Being a sea loch, Loch Glencoul is tidal and with the tide gradually going out since we arrived at Kylesku, more of the rocks lining the edge of the loch had become exposed. There lying amongst these seaweed covered rocks were several common seals. As the boat got closer they began to move around and it was then that we saw they were accompanied by their tiny adorable little pups. The females mate at sea in early autumn and have one pup in June or July, which suckles for about a further month so these pups were no more than a month old. Unlike our other British seal, the Atlantic grey, common seal pups can swim almost from birth and go to sea on the next tide. I call the common seal the pretty one as its rounded head, short muzzle, 'v'-shaped nostrils and placid disposition make it an attractive animal whereas the grey seal has a long pointed head, roman nose and is very noisy and aggressive, the exact opposite.

As the boat chugged on we said goodbye to the baby seals and wished them luck, for to survive in the harsh environment of the Atlantic they would need it. Our interest in the natural world was soon replenished by the excitable cries from the so-called swallows of the sea. Three 'commic' terns were diving into the still waters of the loch and emerging with small silver-coloured fish that are the young of several species known as fry. They often hover like kestrels waiting for their prey to rise close to the surface before plunging at great speed into the chilly northern waters. The term 'commic' tern is used by ornithologists when positive identification between arctic and common terns is nigh on impossible, especially at a distance. But these little birds were positively obliging when first one then all three landed on some rocks within binocular range. The short red legs and all red bill were clearly visible proving that these were arctic terns, one of the most travelled birds in the world. For these delightful birds breed on and around the coasts of the Arctic Ocean and the North Atlantic and migrate south to spend our winter in the Antarctic summer. Arctic terns can cover some 20,000 miles a year on migration alone and as some birds can reach twenty-five years of age or more the mileage in their lifetime may exceed a trip to the moon and back. Because of this they are credited with enjoying a greater amount of daylight than any other bird.

As the tide continued to recede large areas of kelp became exposed moving to and fro with the current, a moving khaki coloured carpet. Suddenly a whiskered head appeared within this floating forest some twenty-five yards ahead. I initially thought it was a seal but as it dived beneath the surface the body was followed by a long thin tail. Another eagle-eyed passenger had also spotted this tell-tale sign and yelled out 'otter'. This was immediately followed by the sound of many feet as the majority of the other passengers rushed over to that side of the boat for a better look. I had visions of the boat turning turtle as the majority of the weight was transferred to one side of the boat. I need not have worried as the vessel was substantial enough and unbelievably some people weren't even interested in seeing an otter. It made one further brief appearance before disappearing amongst the kelp never to be seen again. Although we were only treated to a fleeting glimpse the heavy head, thick neck and large size was reminiscent of a male or dog otter that was most probably patrolling his territory and hoping for a bite to eat at the same time. He would move silently on now to the next patch of tangled fronds of the forest kelp hunting for unsuspecting crabs, molluscs and butterfish, as otters and crowds of people do not mix. Perhaps he might be lucky and catch a favourite, the lumpsucker, which is quite large and makes a rather substantial meal. The lumpsucker is a strange fish with its distinctive stout body and a pelvic fin that has been adapted to form a suction disc that enables the fish to attach itself to rocks. The butterfish in contrast has a long slender body with a long dorsal fin made up of short spines. The mucous-covered skin is slippery to the touch and is very difficult to handle but the otter with its dexterous forepaws seems to have little trouble.

To reach the head of the loch we had to pass through a narrow passage of water caused by several small islands jutting out from the northern shoreline. These resembled large stepping-stones put there by an imaginary giant to allow him to cross the loch without getting his feet wet. The loch then opened up again and as we cruised towards the beach where the river waters mixed with the saline loch, the waterfall suddenly came into view. Although it was about a mile away and unfortunately not in spate because of the lack of heavy rain, it was still magnificent. Drained from the wild upland moor the peaty waters cascaded over the rocky terrain to form ringlets of sparkling water droplets – hence its name The Maiden's Tresses. The boat sat there for what appeared to be an eternity as the other passengers took photographs, but I was in a different world. My mind was visualizing the wild place that stood before me and beyond - the rounded top of the Stack of Glencoul and the corries of Glas Bheinn in the foreground and past the falls through to the lochan strewn foothills of Ben More Assynt and Conival. A wild and rugged place that stirs the emotions.

As the boat turned to start its return journey something caught my eye that I can only describe as the icing on the cake. For there soaring high above this desolate but beautiful landscape was not one but a pair of golden eagles. I silently gestured to my wife for I did not want this moment to be ruined by the excited hoards for by now the eagles had moved even further off and were mere dots on the horizon.

On approaching the small islands a pair of ravens flew over the bows of the boat cronking in excitement and relief that their parental duties had finished for this year as by now their youngsters would have fled, for ravens nest very early in the year.

Once through the narrow passage between the nearest island and the shore we headed for the northern shoreline where the terrain rose steeply to a 1500 ft. plateau. These steep slopes were interspersed with rocky outcrops which when joined together formed small cliff faces. Placed precariously on some of the narrow ledges were several large oval nests watched over by tall grey and white sentries with dagger like yellow bills. This is what amounts to a northern Highland heronry. Many of the passengers could not believe what they were seeing for most heronries are usually full of birds and located in an array of tall trees. The lack of trees in this barren landscape means that the heron has no choice but to build its large nest of sticks and twigs on exposed cliffs and to rebuild every year because of the adverse weather in this part of the country.

The rest of the journey was pretty uneventful until we were in sight of our starting point, the tiny hamlet of Kylesku. At first I thought it was a cormorant, as they are pretty common around these parts, but then I realized it was one of only four species of diver in the world, the red-throated diver. We are fortunate to have all four in this country for the red-throated and black-throated are present all year, the great northern is a visitor to our coasts in the winter and the white billed is a rare vigrant. This bird was in full breeding plumage of a wine red throat with matching red eyes contrasting with a velvet grey uptilted head. It dived almost immediately and resurfaced some way off for they are very efficient under water and can catch fish as deep as thirty feet. Although a good swimmer both on and below the surface and superbly streamlined in flight it has, like all divers, the disadvantage of having its legs set far back on its body. This makes it difficult to land and more importantly to walk; hence their nest site is situated close to the waters edge and is susceptible to flooding in heavy rainfall.

The boat gently slid in next to the slipway and was securely tied up before the passengers were allowed off. I held Bracken back until the last passenger had alighted for I could feel her love of boats had waned slightly and terra firma beckoned. She dragged me over the gunwale of the boat again and headed for the vehicle in the car park. We would give her a walk in one of her favourite woods near home as recompense.

On reflection the boat trip was interesting and we did see the seal pups and some great bird life but next time I think the six mile round trip on foot from Loch na Gainmhich would be more exciting, for the wilderness of Eas Coul Aulin should really be reached on the rough heathery tracks of this silent and remote landscape of impressive beauty - but this perhaps is another story.

Chapter 6

FROM SILVER SEA TO
MOUNTAIN SCREE

DIPPER

North-west Sutherland is not renown for its deciduous woodlands, or any woodlands for that matter, but there are a few small isolated pockets clinging to a meagre existence, usually alongside a river course which is protected from the harsh elements that are common place in this area. One such place is a small area of birch, rowan and willow that follows the River Kirkaig from its source at Fionn Loch through to the sea at the small hamlet of Inverkirkaig, just south of Lochinver.

The walk which starts from a small car park situated just outside the village is unique in so much that it contains three totally different experiences. Firstly one of the finest bookshops in the Highlands nestles within the woods adjacent to the beginning of the walk and this is followed by a spectacular waterfall further up the track which in turn leads to magnificent views of Suilven, the mountain known as the Sugar Loaf, across the still waters of Fionn Loch.

This was where I was heading one early summers' day. From my home I first headed north-west on the Ullapool road, then north past Inchnadamph before heading west along the shores of Loch Assynt to Lochinver. Loch Assynt can be a rough and wild stretch of water but not on this day, a slight breeze was just disturbing the surface and as an added bonus was keeping the midges at bay. Just past the crumbling remains of Ardvreck Castle, which sits on a grass-covered promontory that juts out into the loch, I pulled into a small parking spot above the tranquil waters. The view down the loch with the castle in the foreground and the quartzite peaks of Conival and Braebag stretching into the distance was superb. A pair of oystercatchers broke the silence as they piped their annoyance at a couple of common gulls as they foraged around the rocky shore just below the castle and a common sandpiper called as he bobbed from stone to stone along the same shoreline. As I was watching a pied wagtail with a beak full of insects flitting around the front of the Land Rover my eyes were drawn to a disturbance at the waters edge towards the ruined castle. Through my binoculars I could see a small bird rummaging around the stones that formed part of the gravel bed of the mountain burn that ran into the loch. A small sandy beach had been formed on the northern side of the causeway leading to the castle and the bird was swimming underwater in the shallows with the occasional emergence onto a convenient rock before repeating the procedure. The behaviour suggested a dipper and this was confirmed when it suddenly flew closer to resume its feeding habit in a nearby bay. The dipper has the remarkable ability to seek its food by actually walking underwater where it searches for insects, larvae and worms. After catching a tasty morsel it bobbed up and down a few times whilst perched on a large stone before flying back towards the river mouth and disappearing along its course. Obviously a nest and hungry youngsters awaited its return.

A few hundred yards past Ardvreck Castle the road forks at Skiag Bridge with one road climbing through the hills to Kylesku and my road following the contours of the 250ft (80m) deep Loch Assynt. It was difficult to know in which direction to look, for on one side the calm water of the loch was glinting like so many jewels as the sun caught the slightest movement, or to the other with the three mile long western ridge of the mighty Quinag towering above me. Like with many Highland lochs the small islands within them are inaccessible to sheep or deer and are covered with Scots pine, birch and willow scrub as all the surrounding land would have been many years ago. These islands are invaluable as reasonably safe breeding areas for red and particularly black-throated divers who are easily disturbed by man's activities. Some even have the occasional otter holt concealed beneath a hollow tree root or within a jumble of large boulders.

As I was driving along the foothills of Quinag I was suddenly aware of being followed. I glanced to my right - I was confronted with three large black birds flying at head height as if escorting the Land Rover out of their territory. I had seen ravens on many occasions before but not from this angle. The recognisable features of the stout heavy bill and shaggy throat feathers, coupled with the prominent diamond shaped tail as they veered away, was great to see at such close and unusual quarters. It was along this road last spring that I saw a young raven being fed by its attentive parent. Its bright red gape stimulated the parental urge to fill it to capacity even though being close to a road and potential danger.

Leaving Quinag behind, the undulating road eventually started to drop down to the village of Lochinver. This is a busy and thriving fishing port which comes to life later in the day when the fishing boats arrive to unload and sell all their catch from the pier, accompanied by the continuous cries of the resident herring gulls. After crossing the bridge that spans the River Inver the road follows the contours of Loch Inver itself, which in turn is lined with the old village houses displaying decorative B & B signs, as this is a popular tourist area. Since my visit a brand new Assynt Visitor Centre has been opened which provides the tourist with information on the area, accommodation details, books, maps and visual habitat displays. One such display is a scaled down model of a cliff face complete with nesting seabirds. Superbly modelled in exacting detail the puffins, razorbills, guillemots, kittiwakes, fulmars and shags are accompanied by a tape of the calls and sounds that contribute greatly to the life-like exhibition. All that is needed is the distinctive smell of guano to complete the scene.

Once past the village the road forked to the right onto the pier, fish market and the famous Culag Hotel and to the left over the picturesque River Culag and on to Inverkirkaig. From the bridge the road narrowed considerably to become very much single-tracked with passing places at strategic points which were needed to negotiate the twists and turns as it rose high above the distant coastline. The first couple of miles were extremely tricky with many blind corners and bends and I spent most of my time watching for on-coming traffic or the inevitable wandering ewe or lamb or both. Although great concentration was needed this did not distract from the enjoyment of the drive as the road meandered past small croft houses, some long since renovated, nesting in every nook and cranny that gave some form of shelter from the prevailing south-westerly wind. The road levelled out across bare moorland before dropping down to the sheltered bay at Inverkirkaig village, where a small raft of male eiders bobbed just off the pebbled beach.

As I turned inland at the end of the small hamlet the landscape instantly changed as I followed the course of the River Kirkaig. Instead of coarse heather the river bank was lined with alders, willows and birch trees. Not being at the height of the tourist season, the small car park at the beginning of the walk was only half full, so I was able to park the Land Rover with ease. I was instantly joined by a host of chaffinches, a couple of blue tits and a great tit, all hoping for their elevenses. I threw them a few pieces of bread from my lunch, slung my rucksack on my back and armed with my thumbstick and binoculars crossed the road to begin the walk. I have used a thumbstick now for many years and find it particularly useful when walking up steep inclines or clambering over rough terrain, especially as ano-domini catches up. Three legs are always better than two and although the walk is not long, it is quite demanding.

Once through the small side gate next to the high deer gate, the wide vehicle track gave way to a small path within a hundred yards or so. This well-trodden path passed through two further gates to wind through the deciduous woodland that followed the course of the fast flowing river. In this kind of environment sound is the predominate sense that some people, especially towns folk have forgotten how to use. The background was dominated by the sound of the river as the turbulent waters broke against enumerable boulders clinging to the river bed and squeezed between crevices to form tranquil eddies where small brown trout rested before resuming their feeding pattern amongst the moving water. This was where a grey heron suddenly alighted as my innocuous movement was spotted by this most nervous of birds. It had been hunting in one of those small pools near the rivers edge concentrating totally on stalking the unwary fish fry when self-preservation kicked in.

My favourite habitat is deciduous woodland and even this narrow stretch contained many interesting sights and sounds. Willow warblers sang from the tops of birch and willow, blue tits chittered through the branches along with the mimicking calls of the great tit, and blackbirds turning over the leaf litter for worms suddenly scurried off amidst deafening alarm calls. But despite all this one bird song stood out amongst all others, the melodious wood warbler. Not numerous by any means, especially this far north, it is recognized more by its song than its appearance. With yellowish-green upper parts and a sulphur yellow breast and being a member of the so-called leaf warblers, this elusive bird is very difficult to spot being hidden by the foliage amongst the tree canopy. Luckily he has a very unforgettable song that has two phases. The first is a series of single notes accelerating into a trill that is repeated regularly. The occasionally heard second phase is series of plaintive 'pew-pew-pew' notes growing gradually fainter. Complimenting this distinctive song was a handsome male redstart flitting through the rowan and birch trees uttering his anxious 'wee-tic-tic' alarm call accompanied by the less colourful female.

Once through this oasis of woodland, the path that appeared to be cut into the hillside wound its way through deer grass and heather following the course of the river. In contrast the other side of the river continued to be clothed in a green mantle of stunted mixed woodland that was protected from the prevailing wind by the steep sides of the gorge. Because of the nature of the terrain rocky outcrops broke the pattern where trees and bushes were unable to secure a tenuous foothold. These were where red deer suddenly appeared as they broke cover to reveal their presence previously being unnoticed camouflaged against the foliage. Most were young stags that form bachelor herds at this time of year before joining the hinds in the autumn. How nice it was to see red deer where they belong, browsing through the ground litter of mixed woodland where their ancestors began their existence, for red deer are true forest deer that have adapted to life on the open hillside.

From here the path began to leave the rivers edge and climb rapidly up the adjoining hillside. The higher you climbed the rougher the path became. Huge boulders that had been exposed by the erosion of many trampling feet and the washing away of the under-soil in heavy rain had to be negotiated, along with nature-made bridges over sparkling burns which had made their way down from hill lochans into the river below. Once away from the river and woodland the silence was deafening broken only by the haunting cronk,cronk of a passing raven. When I am walking in the hills and nothing has stirred for some time you can bet a large black bird with a fanned tail will appear to break the monotony. The silence was broken a second time by two buzzards circling over the wooded area with primaries outstretched mewing in perfect harmony.

After a steep two hundred feet climb the stony path leveled out to become more natural snaking its way through boggy sphagnum moss and deer grass bordered by the purple flowered, insect-eating common butterwort. The roar of the falls signalled my arrival at my destination with the sound of crashing waters drawing me towards the edge like a magnet. It was a magnificent sight. The high spring rainfall in the area this year had left the hill lochs with plenty of surplus water, so the river, although not in spate, had plenty of spirit as it approached the head of the falls. I had decided to have my lunch overlooking the falls and after inspecting the subsequent terrain bordering the gorge I discovered a small grassy plateau encased within a high rocky outcrop. Fallen bounders supplied nature's table and chairs and it seemed an ideal spot for a bit of rest and relaxation.

Although unable to see the falls from my vantage point the roaring sound obliterated any other background noise enabling the mind to concentrate on the simple things. How old is this rock I am sitting on - how does that tree survive with its roots buried into that crevice -where does that beetle live? Suddenly my thought pattern was interrupted by a large shadow being cast over the sun. I looked up to see this huge dark bird with primaries outstretched disappearing behind me. I jumped up and with half my lunch disappearing over the edge of the ravine to supplement the diet of the local wildlife, I grabbed by binoculars just in time to see a magnificent golden eagle disappearing over the next ridge. What an awe-inspiring bird it is, a six foot wingspan, three feet from its formidable beak to tail and with talons large and lethal enough to kill a red deer calf. Having retrieved what was left of my lunch from the surrounding foliage I disappeared into my subconscious to recall my many encounters with golden eagles. From the most unforgettable in the foothills of Inchnadamph where it was so low I could clearly see the golden crown, to the dog-fight between eagle and peregrine in the skies above Glencalvie. Memorable times indeed, never to be forgotten.

Snapping back to reality I collected all my belongings and decided to continue a little further to the enclosed waters of Fion Loch. The path now tracked the flow of the river, which began to widen and reduce its ferocity. This in turn produced small eddies along the edge where silver spangled water danced through a maze of multi-coloured rocks. Adorning these rocks were a couple of birds strangely called grey wagtails whose most predominant colour is a striking sulphur yellow. These dapper little birds whose tails never stopped bobbing were searching between the rocky crevices for small insects and invertebrates. As if to compliment the wagtails the sudden arrival of an adult dipper really made my day. Its characteristic low direct flight from the vicinity of the loch was in total contrast to many other water birds except the lowland kingfisher. After submerging in the cool waters and literally walking on the river bed to catch unsuspecting insect larvae it emerged onto a lichen covered boulder only a few yards from me. I immediately stood completely still as any sudden movement would make it disappear further up the river. With my camouflage clothing enabling me to blend in with the surrounding terrain I was able to watch it for some time. It stood on the boulder with the clear water lapping around it and started to preen. Firstly under its short stubby wings then through its white chest to the contrasting chestnut waistband. Having given itself a wash and brush-up it then carried on as only dippers can, repeatedly bobbing up and down on stiff legs with white eyelids blinking in unison before flying off further upstream. As if this wasn't enough excitement, another dipper suddenly appeared on the far bank but this time it was a young bird easily recognizable by its grey-brown upper parts and speckled white below. The parents must have constructed their bulky, domed nest beside or actually behind the waterfall as they have a preference for this type of habitat when nesting. I was virtually at the end of my walk as the path meandered its way to the lochside, where a small, clinker built rowing boat was moored nearby nestling in a tiny sheltered bay. This boat is used by estate workers to reach the far side rather that traverse the head of the loch on the continuing path. I now stood on a small heather strewn promontory with the dark waters of the loch before me and the mass of Suilven stretching up into the sky, how insignificant I felt.

The mountains in the far north-west Highlands are unique. Normally the mountains throughout the Highlands consist of a conglomeration of individual peaks forming a range of high hills over a large area, but the mountains of Assynt and Inverpolly are different. They rise in strange isolation from a heather and peat bog landscape in a variety of individual shapes that are easily recognizable to the discerning mountain lover. To the south-east the quartzite-capped twin summit of Cul Mor and her smaller sister mountain the pyramidal Cul Beag, form a unique triangle with the pinnacled and shattered crest which is the small but beautifully formed Stac Polly. All three lie within the incredibly wild but beautiful Inverpolly nature reserve in Wester-Ross. The distant skyline of the north-east is dominated by the long and forked ridge mass of Quinag with its three summits rising in a 'Y' formation. In the west and standing at 2779 feet (only seven feet lower that Cul Mor) the most shapeless of mountains in the region of Assynt is the sandstone wedge of Canisp. In total contrast it's dominating near neighbour is the spectacular Suilven. Despite its comparatively modest height of 2399 feet it is the most easily recognizable mountain in the area. Its remarkable outline produces a different semblance when viewed from different angles. From the west a massive thimble, from the east a slender pinnacle, but from where I was standing its full beauty was revealed. Her rounded dome is ringed by precipitous cliffs and linked by a narrow ridge that dips in the middle to form a saddle before rising through a deep cleft to a sharp towering peak. The only way to climb this spectacular mountain is to ascend the steep zig-zag path to the saddle of Bealach Mor, which bisects the crest of the summit ridge. From here a well-trodden path passes through an unbelievable well-built stone dyke (wall) to the summit of Caisteal Liath. Why this dyke was constructed across the ridge is open to speculation.

It was while I was standing there, transfixed before this magnificent effigy to the wildness of the Highlands that the final piece of the jigsaw depicting my exploration slotted into place. For there, soaring between the two pointed tops which form the eastern end of Suilven was the unmistakable shape of a golden eagle. The perfect compliment to a majestic mountain.

Chapter 7

AN ISLAND EXPERIENCE

THE GREAT STACK - HANDA ISLAND

Outward Bound

May is one of the best months in the Highlands for good weather, nature watching and enjoying the countryside. The hills still have the last remnants of the winter snows, the trees are bathed in fresh new growth and wild flowers are waking from their enforced sleep – expectation is in the air.

I had decided to make my usual pilgrimage to Handa Island, the bird reserve off the north west coast of Sutherland. The journey from my home to the nearest point on the mainland and the return entails travelling through some of the wildest yet excitingly beautiful scenery throughout the northern Highlands.

After travelling along the Kyle of Sutherland past the stately Carbisdale Castle, the road rises to reveal the panoramic views of Strathoykel with the much revered salmon river, the Oykel, flowing into the Kyle from its hill source in the far distance. Continuing through the market town of Lairg the road bears left along Loch Shin. This loch is approximately 18 miles long and coupled with lochs Merkland, More, and Stack virtually joins the Atlantic with the North Sea. A few miles along Loch Shin a piece of land juts out into the loch producing an inlet. It's always worth stopping the Land Rover and having a detailed look through the binoculars and this time I was not disappointed. I could not believe my eyes, swimming nonchalantly in single file were a pair of barnacle geese. These geese should have been further north by now but had obviously decided to break their long journey and reward me with a rare sight for this particular part of the country.

A couple of miles further on and approaching Loch Merkland I could just hear the muted plaintive cry of a red-throated diver over the drone of the Land Rover engine. Having parked the vehicle in a convenient lay-by I scoured the loch and there lying very low in the water was the bird I was looking for. It raised its head and stretching its neck forward let out its mournful wail, which echoed around the surrounding hills interrupting the natural silence of the wilderness. Suddenly there was a further red throat, this time descending rapidly to the loch, skimming its surface and landing on its belly water ski fashion, within twenty yards of its obvious mate. Apart from the sharp kwuk-kwuk-kwuk call in flight which it shares with other divers, the wail is the birds only other voice. This most musical territorial call is said by the locals to herald rain and therefore they named this most elegant of birds the "rain goose".

Approaching Achfary the eyes are drawn to the beautiful situation of this picturesque little village nestling in between the arms of the single pinnacled Ben Stack and the sandstone scree slopes of Ben Arkle. A truly green oasis with rhododendron bushes enclosing the wooded lodge grounds and the unusual formal gardens of Achfary House complimenting the black and white estate buildings. Even the telephone box is painted black and white, this being the only non B.T. coloured box in Great Britain.

This north-westerly corner of the British Isles is also the stronghold of the magnificent black-throated diver. To see this rare bird in its spectacular breeding plumage involves taking a small detour. I approached the remote loch with trepidation, will they be there or not! As I rounded the bend on the single-track road I was intrigued by the strange calls coming from around the point. Stopping the Land Rover I assumed the commando position – flat on your belly. Carefully I edged forward hoping my green attire would camouflage my shape against the heather and grasses of the otherwise featureless landscape. Peering through the razor sharp leaves of a high mound of tussock grass I was amazed at the sight that confronted me. Not one pair of black throats but eight individuals, all milling around one another making an excited chittering noise. Having never seen or heard this before I can only assume that it is a group of local birds pairing up and discussing the availability of breeding territories for the coming season. Sure enough, after about five minutes, six of these beautiful birds took flight leaving the resident breeding pair to display to each other and hopefully produce the customary two young. There is no finer sight than fluffy chicks riding on mothers back with father in attendance, dwarfed by the backdrop of one of Sutherlands' finest mountains.

In Britain black-throated divers breed only in Scotland and with evidence of a recent population decline number about 150 breeding pairs, making it twice as rare as the golden eagle. There are many reasons for this decline, increased human activity on some of their breeding lochs, conifer afforestation and water level fluctuations. Some say black throats are easily disturbed but I have witnessed breeding successes year after year on lochs regularly used by fishermen, provided there are small islands for them to nest on. One of the ways that the RSPB are helping to alleviate some of the problems is to make artificial islands, secured to the bed of the loch by a flexible chain. This enables the island to rise and fall with the change in water levels brought about after heavy rain, which would normally have flooded the island and destroyed the nest site. All divers are designed for swimming under water and have their legs positioned well to the rear of their bodies therefore making it very difficult for them to walk and take off. Because of this they have to nest very close to the waters edge and need unobstructive lochs, which make them very vulnerable to lochside conifer plantations and flooding. Let us hope with a little help and give and take, these magnificent birds will adorn the remote northern Highland lochs forever.

Returning to the main route we come to the Laxford Bridge junction. Visitors are amazed as they expect a large iron construction carrying the main road north to the busy fishing port of Kinlochbervie, but instead are confronted by a rather insignificant stone bridge spanning a small river of the same name.

The road south to Scourie occasionally skirts the coast revealing another of the unique features common only to north-west Sutherland. The coastline, sea lochs and inland lochs are studded with small islands made up of pink sandstone sparsely covered with moss and lichens. Some of these islands are inhabited by nesting gulls, shags, cormorants and eider ducks in the breeding season, with the very small islands used as sun loungers by the basking common and grey seals.

A further couple of miles along the road is the turn off to Handa

Island. Over the cattle grid and you enter another world. The small single track road that winds up, down, and around, past loch after loch has to be driven along cautiously, though the temptation to glance left and right hoping for a glimpse of the odd diver or otter is irresistible. Eventually the steep descent to the tiny hamlet of Tarbet is reached. It's as though you have stepped into a time-warp – small croft houses dotted around, sheep on hill and road, pond nestling at the bottom of the hill enhanced by a covering of water lilies, the quacking of domestic ducks, and chickens of all sorts scurrying around feeding on insects, worms and wild seeds as their ancestors used to. The only reminder of progress is a conveniently placed 'loo' and a small croft house converted into a seafood restaurant.

The Island

After having parked the Land Rover on the grass, which is used as an overspill car park during the spring and summer, I walked the short distance carrying my rucksack, binoculars and telescope, to join the ferry queue at the jetty. There were about half a dozen people in front of me but knowing that the boats hold eight or nine I would make the first with room to spare. Having to wait for the boat on its return journey from the island gives you an opportunity to pass the time of day with your fellow passengers and explore your immediate surroundings. The small cliffs on either side of the tiny cove make this an ideal natural harbour and being relatively sheltered the water was exceptionally calm and clear, enabling detailed inspection of the sandy bottom. Scurrying about were crabs of all different sizes being joined the shoals of small fish, all after an easy meal from the discarded fish and lobster waste entangled in the ochre coloured seaweed. On the shingle beach the dapper little black and white pied wagtail was searching for insects amongst the stranded seaweed and debris with a solitary wren singing his territorial song from the surrounding willow scrub – so much volume for such a little bird.

At last the boat arrived, a sixteen footer, clinker built with a small Japanese outboard and certainly showing her age. As we climbed aboard I asked the young boatman what the crossing was like. "A bit splashy" was the reply, said with a slight grin. Although it was a fine, bright, sunny day, the moderate south westerly wind coupled with the incoming tide could make the ten minute crossing very interesting. Once past the shelter of the mainland the passage between it and the island is notorious for its swirling currents and can be extremely hazardous at times. Ignoring my advice to slip on wet weather gear, some unsuspecting passengers clambered for the front seats of the boat, but with my past experience I headed for the stern. With the boat full the small outboard roared into life and away we went. As we left the shelter of the natural harbour two large greater black-backed gulls were standing on some large rocks either side of the exit, like two sentries waiting for a password to allow us through. The first part of the journey was quite uneventful weather-wise allowing us to enjoy very close views of the delightful black guillemot. This little bird in its summer plumage of overall black with white wing patches, red legs and gape, resembles the common guillemot in shape but nothing else. The black guillemot, often called by its Nordic name 'tystie', unlike its larger cliff ledge breeding relative, lays its two eggs under boulders or in rock crevices near the base of a cliff. In Britain it breeds only in Scotland and Ireland and whilst other auks winter out at sea, most tysties stay near their breeding areas.

The main channel between the island and the mainland was a bit more choppy with the waves splashing over the bows of the little boat and the engine struggling to make headway against the force of the incoming tide. Peering through my water spotted spectacles I could see the passengers who insisted on sitting at the front of the boat without any protection were huddled together against the elements and extremely wet. Approaching the island on the leeward side the sea calmed dramatically and we were able to enjoy the picturesque welcoming scene of Handa Island. The boat was heading for a small white shell-sand beach being daily washed by a clear blue-green sea. This coupled with the sun, which had just poked its head out on cue could have been mistaken for one of many small pacific islands – apart from the temperature! Activity was all around us – small groups of male and female eider ducks bobbing on the sea like barges, shags flying as straight as arrows barely a few inches above the waters surface, common and arctic terns hovering and dropping like stones to catch small fish, great and arctic skuas cruising on the thermals above the high cliffs and the kwuck-kwuck of a passing red-throated diver completing the magical scene. The boat is beached literally, with multi coloured milk crates placed upside down in a line like stepping stones to enable passengers to disembark, as there is no jetty on the island. Once ashore there is a short walk through the sand dunes to the bothy where the warden was waiting to welcome us and give a resume of the islands' history and what species of birds and wild flowers are likely to be seen.

The island is owned by Major and Dr. Balfour of Scourie Estate and has been a nature reserve managed by the RSPB since 1962, although in 1992 the management was taken over by the Scottish Wildlife Trust. The island covers 766 acres of mostly rough pasture and peat bog and this national and internationally important site for breeding seabirds is designated as SSSI. The island was once home to about 60 people who led a Spartan existence until their departure in 1848 after the onslaught of the potato famine. The remains of their croft houses can still be seen but the crumbling walls are now home to nesting wheatears. Below the ruins lie the indentations of the lazy beds where potatoes and oats were grown which now, undrained and overgrown, are ideal for the elusive snipe. This bird is best seen during its courtship display when it climbs to over fifty feet on rapidly beating wings and then dives giving out a plaintive bleating sound caused by its vibrating outer tail feathers. It then repeats the performance for anyone who missed it the first time. Once past the ruins the narrow but well-worn path continues its boulder strewn incline across the island's interior that is dominated by deer grass, heather and purple moor grass. The boggy areas are enriched by the colour range from white to deep purple of the heath spotted orchid and the insectivorous butterworts and sundews that are widespread. From here on the main thing to look out for are the nesting skuas. Two species breed on the island's moorland, the great skua or bonxie, a large powerful predator about the size of a herring gull and the arctic skua, which is smaller with a lighter build. Both are pirates and will feast on both eggs and young of the neighbouring seabirds and also harass them into disgorging their hard earned meal. Both defend their territories aggressively against each other and human intruders and as the arctic skua tends to breed nearer the path there is a constant threat of being dive-bombed during the breeding season. This is a small price to pay for the privilege of studying these magnificent birds at close quarters either sitting serenely and partially camouflaged in a clump of heather or indulging in spectacular dogfights with each other.

Approaching the north side of the island Swabbie Loch can be seen on the right nestling in a small hollow depression. Occasionally red-throated divers can be seen here at this time of year but are more frequent in late summer accompanied by their chicks, which were bred on the nearby Hill Tarn. The grass covered edge overlooking the 100 ft. drop to Puffin Bay is an excellent place to stop for lunch with the north west coastline stretching out below you and the continual fly past of fulmars for company. Although called Puffin Bay very few puffins actually breed here, even so they can be seen mingling with the many auks, kittiwakes, fulmars and skuas wheeling around the rock strewn bay. The north and west faces of the island are formed of Torridonian sandstone that has weathered into numerous ledges, caves and free standing stacks. The small stack at Puffin Bay appears, if viewed from a certain angle, to be cut out of the cliff and moved into the centre of the bay by a mythical giant.

Approaching the Great Stack the first thing that is indelibly embossed on the mind is the overpowering noise and smell from the many thousands of nesting seabirds. The stack, which lies just off the main cliffs is a high rise tower block for seabirds with puffins nesting in the burrows, excavated on the roof and a couple of pairs of greater black-backed gulls as untrustworthy neighbours. Next are the very striking black and white razorbills tucked in amongst the surrounding boulders. The top story ledges are occupied by the brown and white common guillemots interspersed with the white spectacled northern race termed as 'bridled'. The guillemots being the most numerous of the seabirds pack the ledges shoulder to shoulder, sitting on their single pear-shaped egg that is designed not to fall off the cliff during their frequent squabbling. The middle storey of the tower block is occupied by the very pretty and only true seagull, the kittiwake. This gull, identified by its yellow bill, black legs and pure black wing tips, described as being dipped in ink, is the only member of the gull family to spend all its time at sea apart from at breeding time. The cup-shaped nest made up of seaweed and grass, combined with a mixture of excrement and mud, has the appearance of a manufactured concrete structure. Further towards the base of the stack are a few shags with their nests tucked under rocky overhangs to avoid the descending guano.

Moving away from the bustle and noise of the stack the eye is diverted to the fulmars, nesting in what can only be described as a natural rock garden. Fulmars, preferring the more sheltered depressions and ledges of the main sea cliffs, are surrounded by scurvy grass, roseroot, sea campion and mayweed, whose waxy surfaces and fleshy leaves protect these plants from the harsh environment.

As I approached the highest point of the island my attention was drawn to the magnificent buttresses, which form the opposite cliff face. With the seabirds wheeling around and the waves crashing into the discarded rocks at their base it is a scene to be treasured and remembered. From here the trail is a very gradual descent to the south of the island. The close cropped grass is festooned with thrift nestling between lichen covered boulders that in turn are adorned with dark little rock pipits and wheatears. As the sea cliffs begin to lose their height so the numbers of nesting seabirds diminish but the wildlife experience goes on. The smaller cliff sites are the main domains of the shags, the incubating birds tucked in their untidy nests of sticks and seaweed with the off-duty birds hanging their wings out to dry on the adjoining rocks. Shags have to be seen at close quarters to be appreciated, the iridescent green plumage, sparkling emerald green eye and breeding head tuft, transform a distant dark form into a precious gem. I am now virtually down to sea level having passed several small bays containing small parties of male and female eider ducks and several roman nosed heads of Atlantic grey seals. At this point on the walk a considerable length of wooden duck boarding winds its way across some mossy peat bog interspersed with heather and willow scrub. As I was walking along the boarding I kept seeing something moving between the boards. So I stopped, edged forward gently so as not to cause any vibration and stared in wonderment. There sunning themselves on the warm wood between the slats were numerous common lizards. These reptiles emerge from hibernation early in the spring and need to bask in the sun a great deal at first to re-activate their metabolism because they lack the means of producing and maintaining their own body heat. These delightful little creatures are the typical lizard colouring of dull brown but tinged red, yellow or green with dark back and side stripes. Lizards eat a variety of small insects, particularly spiders, but they themselves also fall prey to many animals and birds even though they have the ability to shed their tail as a diversion while scuttling to safety. Reptiles that bear live young such as the common lizard, slow worm (legless lizard) and adder can bask during pregnancy ensuring fast development of their young. These species can live further north than the grass snake and sand lizard that lay eggs where warmth cannot be guaranteed and the young are therefore slower developing.

After negotiating the duck boarding the trail wends its way back towards a small cove where a ringed plover had made its scrape of a nest, lined with pebbles, on the short turf above the sandy beach. The tranquillity of this peaceful scene was broken by the continual calls of a large flock of kittiwakes who had just risen into the air and were dancing from one small island to another that lie just off the coast. Scanning the water with my binoculars there were many birds diving below the surface for food, mainly shags, eiders and several red-throated divers. But there amongst the red throats was a much larger bird with a very white breast and underparts. After struggling with the tripod, the anticipation making one all fingers and thumbs, the telescope confirmed my suspicions – a great northern diver in full summer plumage. This truly magnificent bird with its heavy bill, black head and neck with distinctive white band on the neck and white spots on its black back, is not usually seen this far south at this time of year. Primarily a North American bird where it is known as the common loon, its European footholds are Iceland and Greenland. The birds that turn up on the north-west coast at this time of year are making their way north after spending the winter around the British and Irish coasts.

After spending some time wrapped up in the euphoria of watching this rare sight I had failed to notice the wind getting up and the small white horses appearing on the surface of the sea in the less sheltered channels between the mainland and the island. The path now winds its way through bracken and heather to rejoin the path I started on at the ruined crofts. It is only a short distance past the sheep pens to the rise above the day shelter where I started on of the most spectacular and exciting walks in north-west Sutherland.

On descending to the day shelter I had noticed that there were several people on the adjoining beach which indicated that because of the state of the tide we would be leaving from this bay rather than the beach we had arrived on in the morning. After a few minutes I could hear the distinctive drone of the outboard as the two boats appeared from around the headland. Both boatmen were wearing their wet weather gear, which seemed a bit strange as there hadn't been a drop of rain all day. Willy, the older boatman, who is most considerate to his passengers, suggested that anoraks were the order of the day as it was a bit rough out there. This statement was followed by a continued frenzy by the passengers to garb themselves with every conceivable combination of nylon over-suits to one woman's insistence to clothe herself in very oversized pvc fishermans trousers and smock. Both boats were full to capacity with myself opting to occupy the rear seat beside the outboard in Willy's boat. I am a great believer in putting my faith in the older and more experienced members of society, especially where seamanship and knowledge of the sea is called for. My fellow passengers consisted of three middle aged married couples including the lady with the trousers, a young single woman and myself. As the outboard spluttered into life and the boat edged its way out of the calm sheltered bay everybody was in high spirits as it had been a marvellous day full of exciting and interesting things to see. This euphoria was soon to change. To get into the main channel we had to go round a small headland that formed part of the semi-circle of the bay. As we were approaching this rocky outcrop the boat began to rise and fall as we encountered the waves formed by the winds effect on the now open sea and the incoming tide. The jovial banter from my fellow passengers had ceased and everyone was stunned into silence as the boat pitched and rolled as the boatman turned side on to the waves to negotiate the headland. Even I was concerned and after all the crossings I had done in all sorts of weather. The small boat with the seats only about a foot from the top of the gunnels, was being tossed around like a cork and the outboard was over-revving as the propeller was being lifted clear of the water. I quickly glanced around the boat, the couples were holding onto each other for dear life, the single person like myself was trying to appear calm and confident, but the woman with the trousers who was sitting in the bows facing me was obviously near to panic and praying out loud. I instantly thought that if we did capsize she would, in that attire, sink like a stone. Willy, the boatman, had a passive expression on his well weathered face, but I could see that he was concentrating on the job in hand. He steered the boat close to the rocks to achieve as much protection as possible from the wind and waves. Once we had negotiated the headland and were practically opposite the beach that we arrived on earlier in the day, the small boat changed character. With the wind behind us and the action of the waves forcing us forward, this glorified rowing boat became a powerful speedboat, cutting through the water at a fair rate of knots. The mood from the passengers suddenly changed back to light hearted vain as the mainland got nearer and nearer. Suddenly Willy spotted a puffin bobbing around on the sea close to the boat and before anyone realised what was happening he had turned the boat back facing into the wind for us to get a better view. Instantly the boat started to buck again. The young single woman, who had up to this time been absolutely silent during the crossing, suddenly yelled out 'to hell with the puffin let's get home'. This sentiment was echoed by all and Willy reluctantly turned the boat round and headed for the jetty. On disembarking there was a feeling of relief in the air as our feet touched terra firma.

Homeward Bound

The ordeal of the sea crossing passed over into my subconscious as I climbed into my safe and secure Land Rover. After a quick cup of tea to steady the nerves I began the initial steep climb from the car park at Tarbet to the main road. The slow but steady progress was rewarded once I had reached the brow of the hill and was passing one of the many inevitable fish farms that inhabit the west coast lochs. There just beyond the cages was a black-throated diver with just his head below the surface of the water peering into the depths trying to spot his next meal. A quick dive and that was the last I saw of him. These birds can dive to a depth of 30 metres and stay submerged for 10 minutes and it is therefore not surprising that with all the small islands that are dotted around the lochs a hunting diver can easily disappear from view.

I had decided to make this a round trip so at the junction with the main road I turned right towards the village of Scourie. On the approach to the village there is a small loch on the right that always has a flock of greater black-backed and common gulls splashing and preening in its centre. Why this phenomenon should be so I do not know, perhaps it has something to do with the loch having a depth of 20 metres and also being 15 metres above sea level, producing cool, clean and fresh water to bathe in.

Scourie is a typical Highland village and is the local metropolis hereabouts with shops, hotel and a small caravan site overlooking the sandy beach of Scourie Bay. The road then winds its way across Eddrachilles Bay with wild mountain and moorland on one side of the road and the bay with its wealth of uninhabited islands on the other. It is said that there is an island for each day of the year. The road now bends slightly inland and over Duartmore Bridge where the stone bridge that carried the old road can still be seen in the distance straddling the narrow part of Loch Yucal. The shallows of the loch between the bridges are sparsely covered in reeds that are visited by wigeon, teal and occasionally red-throated divers. I had decided to stop in the large parking area just before the new Kylsku Bridge. This bridge was opened by the Queen in 1985 and replaced the ferry, which caused chaos in the tourist season due to the long delays both north and south. During the war the surrounding deep waters were used as a training area for the crews of the British midget submarine fleet and it was from here that the flotilla, each towed by a full sized submarine, left for the successful attack on the Tirpitz in the Norwegian Fiord. The scenery from this viewpoint is breathtaking dominated by the huge bulk of Quinag (the water stoup). The mountain with its many summits rises from a plinth of Lewisian Gneiss and is composed of purple Torridonian Sandstone capped with Cambrian Quartzite. The highest of these summits overlooks the three beautiful sea lochs that converge at the base of the bridge. At the head of one of these lochs, Glencoul, lies the highest waterfall in Britain, Eas Coul Aulin. To make this scene complete, common terns splash into the still waters below me accompanied by the ripples of submerging grey seals and a heron squawks its disapproval of my intrusion into its domain. From here the road rises steadily until the summit is reached, sandwiched between the scree slopes of Quinag and Glas Bheinn. This wild mountain road then has a long descent to Skiag Bridge and the fragmentary remains of Ardvrech Castle, nestling on a small peninsular in Loch Assynt. Ospreys used to nest on this site until their extermination by egg collectors in the 1840's and so far they have shown no interest in returning to the old castle.

At the end of Loch Assynt lies the very small village of Inchnadamph where many start their ascent of Sutherland's highest mountain, Ben More Assynt. The lower limestone slopes are famous for their abundance of rare alpine plants and where the remains of the earliest known inhabitants of Scotland along with the bones of arctic animals were found in 1926. Just past the village, small cliffs run parallel to the road and a stop in a convenient lay-by is essential. A herd of about twenty red deer stags were grazing on the lower slopes with their newly growing antlers covered in thick velvet. Stags form bachelor herds after the rut in September and October and stay together until the following autumn. The cliff face towering above the unsuspecting deer is inhabited by a variety of raptors. Ravens also nest on the crags and once their noisy brood have fledged their discarded nest is more often than not occupied by a family of kestrels. I have often been entertained by the silent kestrel hovering just above the rough pasture looking for an adventurous vole, the mewing cry of a buzzard soaring effortlessly on the thermals and also the distinctive call of a peregrine falcon echoing around the hills from a far off nest site.

This main road is sandwiched between the National Nature Reserves of Inchnadamph and Inverpolly, both wild mountainous areas of outstanding raw beauty. Once past Ledmore and the junction to Ullapool the road turns into a single-track tarmac snake wending its way across once open moorland, now carpeted with conifer plantations. These conifers are still quite small at the moment and are therefore still the haunt of short-eared owls and hen harriers. These magnificent birds can be seen quartering the remaining open ground just barely above the heather looking for the prized short tailed vole or taking the occasional young meadow pipit. These birds like many others, are under threat from the conifer invasion. Once these trees reach a certain height the underlying vegetation dies off causing the short tailed vole population to cease and these birds will have lost their main food supply.

Fortunately the Forestry Commission has seen the error of its ways and is becoming more conservation minded by reducing the planting programme. This helps both birds but the hen harrier still has the added problem of persecution by some keepers. Persecution has reached such heights that there are now only an estimated six hundred breeding pairs of hen harriers in the whole of Britain. On the left side of the plantation a small private track to Benmore Lodge is carved into the hillside, only visible by the telegraph poles lining its route. This track skirts one side of Loch Ailsh and leads to the lodge and beyond. The River Oykel, the famous salmon river of these parts, has its source in the hills of Ben More Assynt and runs into the loch before descending eventually into the Kyle of Sutherland at Bonar Bridge some 25 miles away.

Before beginning the long descent to Oykel Bridge, Loch Craggie can be seen nestling in a small depression along side the main road. This loch, which is often festooned by anglers trying to catch the elusive brown trout, has an interesting addition to its geography. A small island, courtesy of the Forestry Commission and the RSPB, sits delicately on the water at one end of the loch. This island is one of the many artificial nesting rafts that have been sited at a variety of lochs throughout the breeding range of the black-throated diver and particularly where they have had poor breeding success. Of all the floating islands sited by the RSPB in the last few years over half are regularly used. With a breeding success of raising only one chick every three to four years the birds using rafts have been over twice as successful. With only 150 pairs of black-throated divers in Britain, hopefully these rafts will prove to be their salvation. Unfortunately this particular island has had nothing on it other than the occasional cormorant. The disturbance by the fly-fishing fraternity and the close proximity to the road are most probably the reasons for the lack of breeding success.

Once past the loch the road descends gradually to Oykel Bridge with magnificent views of the River Oykel meandering its way through the deep-sided glen where buzzards soar, short-eared owls quarter the rough pasture and cuckoos perch on convenient telegraph wires uttering their distinctive call. It is the male cuckoo that announces his presence by the same monotonous note of cuc-coo while the female call consists of a bubbling chuckle. Although after their arrival cuckoos spread out over any kind of habitat throughout the British Isles, the lack of trees this far north enables them to be more conspicuous. The parasitic breeding habit of the cuckoo is well known and the foster home for the young in this area belongs to the meadow pipit.

After crossing over the river at Oykel Bridge the road passes through Strath Oykel to Invercassley and Rosehall. The magnificent Achness Falls are a sort distance from here. Although not high, the width of the cascading water tumbling through two heights of jagged rock is a sight worth seeing. The road then continues to run parallel to the River Oykel until reaching Bonar Bridge and Ardgay, which is where we started our exciting journey to the north-west coast.

Chapter 8

FLOWER OF SCOTLAND

SCOTTISH
PRIMROSE

The weather throughout the Highland spring and early summer had been atrocious, cloud and rain with very little sun. So it wasn't until the middle of July that my wife and I were able to travel to the north coast in search of Primula Scotica - the Scottish Primrose. This tiny native perennial is only found in small pockets on the north coast of Scotland and on the Orkney Islands and flowers from June to August, so time was running out for this year.

Our plan was to travel through Lairg to Altnaharra along the picturesque Loch Naver and River Naver to Bettyhill. From here the main road meanders through miles of desolate peat bog to the small hamlet of Strathy where a short detour leads to the lighthouse at Strathy Point. This is by far the most well-known and easily accessible site where the Scottish Primrose grows in relative abundance. This was going to be quite a nostalgic trip for my wife who hadn't been to Strathy since our holidays when we lived in Hampshire many years ago.

When we set out the weather had broken and it was a warm sunny day at last. With the dog (Bracken) sitting upright on the back seat of the car we steered our way through Bonar Bridge and along the wide new road to Lairg. Lairg, although little more than a village is the great communication centre for the northern Highlands and like Rome all roads from the north, south, east and west lead to it. It is here every August that one of the biggest one-day sheep sales in Britain is held.

The road between Lairg and Altnaharra passes through a land of burn, moor and lochan in all directions apart from the occasional conifer plantation where the uniformity is scarred by sectional felling and replanting. Past the Crask Inn and the giant spectacle of Ben Klibreck the road winds down to Altnaharra, a tiny village dominated by the large hotel of the same name. This hotel was first built around 1815 as a coaching inn and was partly rebuilt and modernised in 1957 to become one of Scotland's most famous abodes for the salmon fishing fraternity.

At the cross-roads on the outskirts of the village I turned right along the twisting shoreline of tranquil Loch Naver. I pulled into one of the many small picnic spots created by endless holidaymakers throughout the years to let us, and the dog, stretch our legs. And did she do just that, haring through the bracken, heather and a small alder copse, which stretched down to a pebbled beach before crashing into the still waters of the loch, much to the dismay of some distant fishermen. It didn't exactly please a pair of common sandpipers who initially arose piping in alarm before settling down further along the shore.

The drive along the lochside and down the River Naver was a nostalgic one remembering holidays of years gone by. The tiny picturesque Caravan Club site perched down by the loch but hidden amongst the trees was still as attractive as ever. The parking spots along the river where we waited for hour upon hour for an appearance of an osprey that allegedly perched on a certain telegraph pole every day to await his meal to come swimming by. We never did see that particular osprey! The unfortunate badger found dead by the side of the road miles away from typical badger habitat. These are some of the memories instilled in the mind. Strathnaver is a very pleasant glen with individual houses but no village as such throughout its entire length. Half way along is the community of Syre where stands Syre Lodge, the house of the infamous Patrick Seller, who was the unscrupulous factor appointed by Sutherland Estates to evict the local people during the Highland Clearances in the 19th Century.

The narrow, winding road suddenly joined the main thoroughfare that soon descended to the bridge over the Naver estuary and on to the straggling village of Bettyhill. The west side of the estuary is quite unique where huge dunes have been created by windblown sand being deposited on the steep slopes of the headland. Bettyhill is synonymous with the Highland Clearances, for it was here that the majority of the evicted crofters of Strathnaver were settled and the atmosphere still conveyed a feeling of hopelessness and tragedy as we drove through the main street. Ironically the village is named after its founder, Elizabeth, Countess of Sutherland.

The last time we passed this way the road to Strathy was very narrow with passing places where curlew and redshank rose and called from the surrounding moorland. An occasional red-throated diver would drift across the surface of one of the scattered lochans that scarred this deserted forbidding landscape. But not this time! The peace and tranquillity had been replaced by large lorries, earth moving equipment, JCB's and a multitude of brightly clothed workmen who were replacing the old road with a wide modern equivalent. Fortunately before too long the road reverted back to the original and after a short distance we followed the signpost to Strathy Point. The tiny tarred track passed several croft houses before coming to an abrupt end at a very small car park, that judging by the farm equipment dotted around doubled as a sheep and cattle station. We decided to have lunch before trekking the long mile to the lighthouse. We were soon to be entertained by several swallows that were swooping gracefully over the rough grassland to catch any unsuspecting rising insects. Also involved in the hunt were pied wagtails whose distinctive black and white plumage was very apparent as they dashed in and out of the reeds and tussock grass. A few blackbirds were competing with some very aggressive starlings for earthworms in the wetter areas of the pasture but most of the starlings were drilling into the ground for leatherjackets or wireworms. Although the starling is undoubtedly the noisy, brash, tear-away of the bird world where flocks in some parts of the country number hundreds of thousands, here in the northern Highlands it is comparatively rare. If located in a tropical rain forest in small numbers the bird's summer iridescent plumage of shining jet black, shot with purple and green, would surely qualify it as a bird of paradise. But the highlight of the lunch stop was the sudden appearance of a couple of twite. They didn't stay very long but the void produced by their departure was soon filled by a beautiful male wheatear flashing his conspicuous white rump and black T-shaped tail pattern as he flew onto a nearby lichen-covered boulder. After catching a few insects he too flew off, presumably to feed his fledglings from a second brood.

After this very entertaining interlude we decided to make our way to the lighthouse. Having previously seen an old sign saying "No Dogs" we placed Bracken on a lead as a precautionary measure as the surrounding pastures were full of black-faced ewes and half grown lambs which can be very skittish and nervous of strangers. As we made our way down the tarmaced track excited human voices filled the air. Turning around we were confronted by a rather large crofters wife wearing a multi-stained pinafore with several attached children appealing for us to stop. It appeared that the sheep were petrified of any strange dog, even one on a lead, and on previous occasions lambs had panicked and run over the cliff edge to their deaths. After some discussion they allowed us to take the car through their gate and on to the lighthouse, provided we kept the dog in the car, to which we agreed. This was ideal, for my wife has a displaced hip and finds it difficult to walk far and leaving the dog in the car on a hot day could have been a problem. What they didn't tell us was the size of the 'sleeping policemen' installed along the track to stop excessive speeding. They were enormous! They were so high that unless you stopped the car with the front wheels on top of the obstacle before slowly dropping down the other side your exhaust and car would soon part company. Having successfully negotiated five of these concrete obstructions we parked the car on the grass verge just below the large grassy knoll that supported the white painted lighthouse and adjacent buildings. Leaving the dog in the well-ventilated car we began our search. It didn't take long to find our quarry, for there lying amongst the well cropped grass of the lower slopes of the knoll was the tiny Scottish Primrose. Once we had found one we began to run around finding first another then another, we became obsessed. Although coming to the end of its flowering season this diminutive mealy-leafed plant was a delight. To get some sort of comparison in size I photographed a group of the pale purple/pink flowers against a yellow buttercup. The buttercup looked enormous. The sighting completed the pair for us, the Scottish Primrose and the Scottish Crossbill, both indigenous and confined only in their distribution to Scotland.

Engrossed within the euphoria of our findings, the sounds of the nearby seabird colonies were nearly lost in the excitement. Suddenly a harsh "uk-uk-uk" cry pierced the air. I looked up and there flying across the narrow expanse of land between two rocky clefts was a great skua (or bonxie as the Shetlanders call them) whose stocky powerful build and aggressive behaviour demands and receives respect throughout the bird world. This one may have been hunting because no sooner had I seen it than it suddenly banked and dived towards the nearest cliff face. The sudden increase in volume from the cries of the kittiwakes suggested that it might well have been after one of their chicks. Bonxies often pluck a defenceless chick from the nest or knock one into the sea where it either drowns or falls victim to the skua's powerful beak. The north coast of Sutherland is much like the coastline of Cornwall, rugged and serrated with stretches of lofty sea cliffs where thousands of seabirds nest. On the west side of the lighthouse promontory a deep geo and arch has been formed by erosion to the cliffs that are continuously subjected to raging seas. This natural setting was encrusted with nesting guillemots, razorbills, kittiwakes and fulmars with the ever-present great skua and his smaller, lighter cousin the arctic skua patrolling overhead. What a sight it was, the whole chasm was full of birds performing aerial displays past the cliff face and through the arch, accompanied by harmonious cries and the pungent smell of guano that invaded the nostrils. We sat there for a while intoxicated by the atmosphere. Suddenly realising that Bracken was still shut in the car we reluctantly made our way back to be welcomed by a wagging tail and slobbery licks. We slowly re-traced our steps over the humps and after thanking the crofter's wife drove back to the main road.

The road continued along the north coast for a few miles before dropping down to Melvich then crossing a bridge over the Halladale River. Once over the bridge we turned right to follow the course of the river towards Forsinard. Our initial plan was to incorporate in our trip a walk around the RSPB reserve at Forsinard but due to time getting on this would have to be done another day and we would have to be satisfied with a look around the visitor centre. As I pulled into the small car park it did appear rather strange as the visitor centre is incorporated within Forsinard railway station. The reserve was acquired in 1995 and covers 17,500 acres of rolling bog land studded with small pools known as dubh lochans. Commonly known as the "Flow Country" these peatlands are breeding grounds for merlins, hen harriers, dunlins, greenshanks, redshanks and golden plovers with red and black-throated divers on the lochans. To our pleasant surprise the farthest end of the centre was devoted to hen harriers with a video link-up to a nest site on the reserve. By this time of year the three chicks were nearly fledged with virtually all their adult feathers apart from small amounts of tell-tale grey down clinging to the dark brown plumage. As we were admiring these fine specimens there was a sudden flurry of activity as the female arrived clutching some gruesome remains in her talons. She dropped the prey and a scuffle broke out between the chicks, each wanting their fair share. She did not stay long, but long enough for us to see what a magnificent bird she was clothed in her dark brown mottled mantle which acts as camouflage when nesting within dense heather. This is in total contrast to the pale grey body and black wing tips of the male's plumage although both have the tell-tale white rump. This family is quite fortunate, as the surrounding moorland is not used for grouse shooting so persecution is reduced and hopefully these parents will rear another brood next year.

A few miles south of Forsinard the road runs parallel with the course of the River Helmsdale, famous for its salmon fishing and royal patronage. For when in the Scottish Highlands Prince Charles and his entourage often descend onto the river in pursuit of the king of fish. The river flows through the Strath of Kildonan to the small fishing village of Helmsdale where small boats still sail from the picturesque harbour bedecked with lobster creels. The strath is most famous for the gold rush of 1869 where about 500 miners flocked to the area to pan for gold in the Kinbrace, Suisgill, Kildonan, Craggan and Torrish burns as well as in the main Helmsdale River.

Bracken had been stuck in the car virtually all day so we had decided to give her a good run at Littleferry near Golspie, so we drove back along the A9 to her most favourite walk, or in her case run, run, run. As we drove into the small car park she began to whimper so I let her out and she quickly disappeared into the nearest sand dunes chasing rabbit smells. That's better I could hear her say! As she was darting from one rabbit hole to another and keeping a watchful eye on us in case we changed direction, we were busy watching a flock of sandwich terns. These, the largest of our regular visiting terns, were screeching in unison as their strong and powerful flight on long narrow wings took them towards the sand-bar at the entrance of Loch Fleet. Throughout the dunes the narrow grassy paths had lost most of their complimentary covering of birds-foot trefoil and wild pansies, but a few remained to tempt the remaining butterflies. Most numerous were the common blues dancing through the marram grass and feeding on one of its favourite plants, the pale pink flowered wild thyme. As we reached a small clearing where one path led into the centre of the dune system and one followed the waters edge, a magnificent sight faced us. The sun had just broken through the clouds and was shining on a particular patch of marram grass where the continual warmth had attracted a multitude of common blue butterflies. There must have been about two hundred resting with wings out stretched, absorbing the sun's rays on the grass stems. In the common blue butterfly species it is the male who has the blue colour with the females being brown but the female also occurs in a blue form with orange markings around the wings. The bright blue colour in the wings actually contains no blue pigment but is produced by the diffraction of sunlight by thousands of corrugated scales that absorb all colours of the spectrum except blue. Although one of the commonest and most ubiquitous butterflies, seeing these vast numbers at one time was indeed a treat to place in the memory bank.

Bracken was really enjoying herself, running in and out of the dunes checking smells and rabbit holes before haring into the shallow waters of the Fleet to cool off. Her exploits disturbed a number of skylarks and meadow pipits with the resident pair of stonechats looking on from afar perched on top of an adjacent tall marram grass stem. Skylarks are declining all over Britain but this area has good numbers that entertain many during the breeding season with their vertical flight and warbling song.

As we approached the end of the dunes system the narrow path widened before dropping down to the beach and during the spring and early summer is a carpet of wild flowers. There are only small remnants left now but these are being replaced by a spiky little plant with basal shaped leaves and a small five petalled star-shaped flower perched on top of a cylindrical tube. Because this particular variety has white flowers this caused much searching through various wild flower books and after much deliberation it was decided that it was a sub-species of autumn gentian although these have pale pink flowers rather than white. This is the most common gentian in the rest of the British Isles but in Scotland it is quite rare, especially with white flowers.

I ran with Bracken along the beach where she splashed through the small pools left by the receding tide and foraged amongst the seaweed for anything edible. Gulls and waders scattered in her wake whereas the nesting eider ducks and cormorants ignored her antics for they were safe on a distant sandbar. Having satisfied her exuberance we returned to the car via the central belt of sand dunes that are interspersed with grass and shingle paths, this gave her a different terrain to explore. After a lengthy drink of water she settled down on the back seat and went to sleep as we drove home. We were all feeling a bit tired and I'm not surprised for at journeys end we had covered over 160 miles just to see a wild flower, but it had been worth it.

Chapter 9

RAPTOR ALLEY

HEN HARRIER (FEMALE)

What attracted me to the Highlands of Scotland was the wild untamed countryside and all the wild creatures that inhabit this remote terrain. The most spectacular and easiest to observe are the birds of prey and the vast array of habitats within Sutherland allows all the British species to be seen. One very good area encompasses the Loch Fleet reserve through to Brora and around to Rogart, which includes the River Brora valley known to local ornithologists as "raptor alley".

I had decided that before driving down the glen I would stop off at one of the best sea watching areas on the south-east coast of Sutherland. After entering the town of Brora I took a small diversion down to the old disused radio station overlooking where the River Brora flows into the North Sea. Due to the increasing interest in ornithology and also with tourism in mind the once community rubbish tip has been converted into a picturesque car park and picnic site by the local council enabling civilised bird watching from a vehicle hide at any time of the year.

I drove the Land Rover into the new car park and positioned myself facing out to sea. It was a clear day, so much so that I could see the Tarbetness Lighthouse close to the horizon with the Moray coast and mountains beyond a shimmering hazy outline in the far distance. Although bright and with good visibility it was rather a cool day, the gentle south easterly wind was in marked contrast to the strong easterlies that seemed to have been blowing for weeks, which is unusual for May. The tide, although quite high, was just beginning to recede with only the largest of the off-shore rocks clearly visible. Judging by the amount of white guano splashes on these boulders they were well used as resting places that was confirmed by the continual to-ing and fro-ing of gulls and cormorants. On one occasion a cormorant and the rarer shag were perched on the same rock, which was a unique opportunity to compare the two. When together the cormorant was much bigger and actually quite brown in colour with those prominent white cheeks, whereas the shag in comparison was a glossy greenish black with an additional short crest which is evident only in the breading season. Suddenly the air was alive with small scimitar winged birds skimming the surface of the water as swallows, house martins and sand martins gauged themselves on the emerging sand flies. In east Sutherland swallows are as common as elsewhere but the house and sand martins only inhabit the area in small numbers, so to see them all together in one spot is quite an unusual but pleasant experience.

Just beyond the members of the swallow family were the other swallows but this time of the sea. Arctic and common terns were flying to and from their breeding colonies further up the coast together with the occasional little tern which nests amongst the more aggressive arctic' for protection. The main reason for the decline in little tern numbers is human disturbance at their favoured breeding sites on sand and shingle beaches, so the safest way to observe the smallest of the tern family is at high or on the ebbing tide when they are feeding in the shallows. After a short wait I was rewarded. It appeared as if from nowhere, hovered then plunged into the shallow water but was unsuccessful. After several attempts, which allowed me to study the bird closely, it caught a small fish and flew off northwards along the coast. The little tern nests in small numbers on scattered beaches north to Caithness but there are fewer than 1500 pairs in the whole of the British Isles. It is easily recognised from other tern species by its size, rapid flickering wing beat, distinctive white forehead and black tipped yellow bill. All the main tern species of the British Isles frequent this area and I was amazed to find all four settled on one of five large boulders that protruded from the sea about twenty yards from the rapidly exposing sandy beach. This was a phenomenal sight, adult common, arctic, little and sandwich terns all perched on one large rock, a novice bird-watchers dream. At this distance the subtle differences between the common and arctic terns were obvious, the shorter legs and all red bill of the arctic compared with the black tipped red bill of the common. When they alighted the extremely long tail streamers of the arctic tern were distinctive and is really the only means of comparison at a distance. Apart from being larger than the other terns, the sandwich tern is easily recognisable by the shaggy crest that adorns its black crown, black yellow tipped bill and black legs. They breed irregularly and usually only in small numbers in east Sutherland but by far the biggest and long established colony in Scotland is at Sands of Forvie in Aberdeenshire.

Just to the north of the car park is where the River Brora flows into the sea and a pebble spit has formed which was covered by a large flock of juvenile and non-breeding kittiwakes with a few herring and greater black-backed gulls adding to the attraction. The black bars in the shape of a 'W' and the black half-collar of the juvenile plumage was very striking compared with the adult kittiwake as they flew around impatiently and landed among the multitude waiting for the tide to recede. The only species of duck around were a few drake mallards sitting with their glossy green heads tucked into their wings and several drake eiders floating around waiting for the water level to drop, making it easier to feed on the small crabs and molluscs that frequent the concealed rocky sea bed. This is where a couple of years ago I had my best view to date of the rare king eider.

It was mid-summer, the tide was on its way in and I had been studying all the resident birds and not expecting to see the king eider as they usually make their appearance around autumn time through to winter. This bird must have been on the other side of the rocky spit and as the water level rose appeared from behind some large rocks following a female common eider and two well grown youngsters. Common and king have been known to mate and breed but I think he was just being paternal. This was the one and only time I had seen the male king eider in full adult breeding plumage, as the previous sightings had all been in the eclipse plumage of mainly brown but still with the distinctive forehead and bill. This bird was so colourful it was like a parrot on the sea. It was quite different from the drake common eider, having a different shaped head, peaked orange forehead, red beak, pale blue/grey head, peachy breast and black back. A real dandy! It is a high Arctic species nesting in north western Russia, Novaya Zemlya and Svalbard and wintering mainly on Norwegian coasts with the odd one or two turning up regularly on the east Sutherland coast between Brora and Dornoch.

As the ebbing tide began to expose more beach, small flocks of waders began to arrive landing just out of sight beyond the radio station. I decided to walk to the end of the stations perimeter fence where I could see the entire stretch of beach. Armed with my telescope attached to the tripod I walked along the sandy path to the end of the chain-linked fence. Flying from a clump of last year's grasses to the barbed wire, which crowned the fence, was a small flock of linnets. A reasonably common bird in southern Britain it is a scarce local resident in the Highlands. They are heavily dependent on weed seeds and therefore frequent areas with plenty of low trees, bushes, scrub and rough grazing which this particular coastal fringe has in abundance. One male was particularly obliging, displaying his handsome breast and pouring forth his persistent twittering song from a convenient concrete fence post. On the seaward side of the path a line of gorse bushes acted as a natural hide to observe the beach stretching out below me. As I was setting up the tripod three ringed plovers flew in followed by what appeared to be two dunlin. One of these was a very pale bird and on further inspection through my binoculars it was obviously not a dunlin but resembled a plover in its actions, although much paler, slimmer and more erect than the familiar ringed plover. After fumbling with excitement to adjust the telescope I was finally able to get a good close up view. It was a plover of some description but unlike the usual plovers that inhabit these shores it had an incomplete black breast band, a black forehead band, a ginger crown with a black bill and black legs. Racking my brain I suddenly thought of a Kentish plover but having never seen one in the wild before I reserved my judgement. Sure enough, a quick consultation with my bird book confirmed it as an adult male Kentish plover. It wasn't until later after copious research that I realised how important this find had been. This bird has never before been seen in Sutherland and since 1949 has only been seen on seven occasions in the whole of Scotland. This scarce spring migrant to the shores of south and south-east England must have been blown across the north sea from its most northerly breeding range in Denmark on the strong easterly winds. Named after the English county where it formally bred, the last nesting record was at Rye Harbour (Sussex) in 1956, although a number of pairs still breed in the Channel Islands. At the first opportunity I reported the sighting and this was later confirmed by two official ornithological recorders who last saw it heading north westerly with two dunlins for company. This rare sighting for the area is now in the record books - fame at last!

The rare plover continued to run about picking up sand flies and small shrimps that were encased within the stranded seaweed abandoned by the receding tide. Suddenly four more ringed plovers and a further two dunlin flew in attracted by the presence of feeding birds. The ever-present ringed plover is one of our commonest small waders and can be seen around the coasts of Britain all year long whereas the dunlin is mainly a winter coastal bird. These dunlin were in their seldom seen adult breeding plumage distinguished by a black belly, red-brown and black back with a brown streaked breast and crown compared with the uniform dull grey of winter plumage. It is very difficult to observe dunlin in their breeding territories due to the stark habitat of poorly drained upland moors with scattered small pools and their excellent camouflage. They are most abundant in the Pennines of northern England and the flow country of Sutherland and Caithness. British dunlins belong to the southern race that ranges north to Iceland in the west and Finland in the east and most winter in southern Europe and North Africa. I find these birds most attractive and coupled with the Kentish plover I was feeling quite pleased with myself.

From the car park it was a short drive past the small harbour at the mouth of the River Brora, which contained a couple of local fishing boats stacked to the gunnels with lobster pots, to the centre of the town. The single-track road then initially follows the river before winding inland to emerge on the shores of Loch Brora. The lower stretches of the river are very popular with fishermen intent of catching the much prized salmon or possibly sea trout that can grow as large as its famous counterpart. At this point after the town bridge, the furthest river bank has been hewn out of thirty feet of vertical rock that is home to a few pairs of fulmars. I once discovered a dark phase fulmar (dark grey/blue head and underparts) which is the arctic race equivalent of our light phase variety, frequenting the rocky ledges but unfortunately it did not find a mate and eventually disappeared.

Once past the few scattered dwellings on the outskirts of the town the road dissects a small area of marshland where the wetter parts have formed small lochans, one of which contains a black-headed gull colony. This colony can be easily seen from the road and as I stopped in the nearest passing place the off-duty birds rose into the air screaming their abuse before settling down once again when they realised I meant no harm. The lochan was very overgrown with rushes and reeds but the small island where the birds were sitting on their platform nests of vegetation was completely surrounded by water even though in parts it only resembled a moat. This protected them from most predators in the area that include fox, stoat and even pine marten, although foxes will swim short distances when there is a chance of a meal. From here to the beginning of Loch Brora on both sides of the road, old birch woods struggle for survival against the swirling tide of sheep, deer and man.

As in most of the Highlands sheep are allowed to roam free and unfenced which puts great pressure on the remaining woodlands where new seedlings are nibbled and new growth curtailed. These introduced hoofed lawn mowers together with the large numbers of wild deer create very old woodland with little or no regeneration that eventually dies never to be replaced. Highland man also adds to the destruction with the general attitude of; when he sees trees he sees only firewood. These views are changing but very slowly.

Loch Brora suddenly came into view as the lochside woodland was replaced by short close-cropped grass grazed by sheep and rabbits alike. The few remaining ancient knarled birch trees that sparsely lined the beginning of the loch were desperately clinging to life. Their roots being totally exposed, like that of the African mangrove swamps, by the erosion of the soil which was continuously washed away when the level of the water dramatically increases after heavy rain in the surrounding hills. The three and a half mile loch is virtually cut into three because in two places only a narrow channel allows the clear water to continue its journey downstream. In this lower of the three lochs a small island sits resolutely in the centre, a living reminder of times gone by, for this island is partially covered in trees. Scots pine, birch, willow, all grow majestically in total contrast to the treeless slopes beyond. A short excursion onto the grass by way of the many tracks that lead to the lochside allowed me to get a good view of the island which was covered not only by trees but by nesting black-headed gulls and a small colony of common terns. For the added protection common terns often nest among the more raucous gulls where the odd lost egg or two is a small price to pay. At one end of the island there sits a large stone cross of Celtic design. It is said that the local people were once buried on islands so that wolves could not dig up their bodies. If this is so it would explain the luxuriant green growth but the more likely reason is lack of grazing. It appears that the much-maligned wolf was exterminated from Sutherland between 1690 and 1700 with one of the last killed in Glen Loth, a few miles north of Brora.

Suddenly I was aware of being watched. What made me turn around I do not know but there flying along the ridge of the hill behind me was a large juvenile golden eagle. The significant amount of white markings on the tail and underwings indicated one of last years young that had survived its first winter, hopefully to continue until the breeding age of five and beyond. After quartering the hill for several minutes using its huge wings effectively to soar and ride the thermals without any apparent effort, it disappeared over the next ridge. A great introduction to 'raptor alley'.

The middle section of the loch is overshadowed by the impressive seven hundred foot sheer face of Carrol Rock with every nook and cranny occupied by nesting fulmars. These birds are beginning to nest further and further inland but I suppose the sea and their feeding grounds are only two flaps and a glide away to a fulmar.

I was just about to continue on my way when I noticed a large flock of birds with several young in attendance strung out in a line, one behind the other, half way across the loch. After a quick look through the telescope all was revealed, they were greylag geese. All the wild geese were by now in their summer quarters but these are descendants of birds introduced into the area in 1937 and have stayed here all year round ever since. To the right of where I had stopped was a small copse of birch and willow that stretched down to the waters edge and through the trees I could see a small bay that was obscured from the road. The calm still waters of the bay were suddenly disturbed as a large object appeared from the depths. My initial though was a cormorant but as the image cleared the unmistakable outline of a red-throated diver materialised. These diving birds make the journey from their breeding lochans far in the hills to feed on the bountiful supply of fish before returning heavily laden.

The last section of the loch is difficult to see from the road as it is hidden by large mature trees that have been planted around Gordonbush Lodge. The road then follows the course of the river where the air was filled with calling oystercatchers, redshanks and curlews as the noise of the Land Rover disturbed them as they prodded and probed the damp rough grassland at the waters edge. This is also buzzard country. I had seen several since joining Loch Brora as the combination of semi-rough pastures, heather and deer grass hillsides and large conifers in which to nest, make this their ideal habitat. I was beginning to become blasé over buzzards when I noticed a flash of a white rump as this particular bird, which was quartering a newly planted conifer plantation high on the hill, suddenly dived into the undergrowth. As it emerged the much longer wings and lack of underwing pattern confirmed it as a hen harrier, either a female or more probably at this time of year a young male, as the plumages are very similar especially from a distance. I watched this birds hunting technique as it subsequently checked every inch of the hillside, until apparently unsuccessful disappeared behind a large stand of mature conifers to renew its moorland vigil elsewhere.

Once over a small bridge the road rose rapidly through another very old birchwood. Sheep and lambs were everywhere and as I slowed to allow two ewes to cross in front of me a distinctive black and white bird flew past the windscreen and onto a nearby branch of a rowan tree. I could see with the naked eye that it was a great spotted woodpecker. There was a convenient pull-in nearby so I stopped facing into the woods and waited. After a few minutes the woodpecker flew to a dead broken tree trunk that had at one time been a magnificent silver birch but was now grey with the passage of time. The large amount of excavated holes bore witness to the amount of woodpeckers that had used it over the years. I could see by the red nape patch that it was a male and after a quick inspection of the well-chiselled hole he flew off into the depths of the wood. The great spotted is the only woodpecker that ventures this far north and this attractive male was obviously checking on his female incubating the pure white glossy eggs within the wooden chamber.

Whilst I was patiently waiting for any further woodpecker activity I noticed a certain amount of commotion in the direction of a ewe who was lying against the trunk of a large old birch tree supporting her relatively new lamb and peacefully chewing the cud. Two small birds were excitedly flitting around her head, chittering their annoyance and obviously aggrieved at her presence. She in contrast was totally oblivious to theirs. When they eventually stayed still long enough I could see that they were a pair of redstarts with beaks full of wriggling insects. They were very upset and disturbed and appeared to be trying to distract the ewe into moving out of the way. But she was quite content and cosy. As the redstarts had not flown off to feed their youngsters elsewhere I wondered whether the presence of the ewe was hampering their approach to the nest. I decided to move the ewe and her lamb on. Once they had moved all was revealed. The ewe had been leaning right across a natural hole in the base of the tree, which was the entrance to a nest consisting of a loosely constructed cup of dead grass and moss. It contained five young of about a week old and as I moved away the parents immediately flew in to feed the hungry brood. My good deed for the day! The male redstart with its richly contrasting colours and distinctive markings is one of Britain's most handsome small birds. Both sexes share its most noticeable feature of a bright russet tail, which is where it gets its name from, as 'start' is Anglo Saxon for tail.

After watching the pair of redstarts going back and forth to the nest several times and with no further action by the woodpeckers I decided to continue onwards. As I reached the summit of the steady incline I slowed to admire the rest of the glen spread out below me. It was then that a small bird the size of a mistle thrust shot past the front of the vehicle and followed the contours of the hillside skimming the tops of the bracken. I grabbed my binoculars and was just quick enough to see the rapidly disappearing bluish grey form and black-banded tail of a male merlin. These shy and rare birds of prey are not often seen as their natural habit of flying low and fast across open moorland and their lack of aerobatic displays, unlike other falcons, make them difficult to spot. As if in consolation for the disappearing merlin a hen harrier, this time a male, suddenly appeared on the far side of the glen. His pale grey plumage with black wing tips stood out in contrast to the dark brown heather clad hillside that he was quartering in search of small mammals and birds. Following a sharp turn and quick dive into the undergrowth he emerged with something in his talons to then return across the moorland to his concealed nest site amongst the heather and bracken.

After the decent to the glen floor a familiar sound greeted me as I stopped to admire a male kestrel perched on an adjacent telegraph pole. A buzzard mewed as it sailed over the neighbouring hillside, circling in the up draught from the hill, keeping a keen eye out for any unsuspecting rabbits. The buzzard relies on the availability of rabbits so much so that in the mid 1950's, when Britain's rabbit population was almost wiped out by the introduction of myxomatosis, the buzzard numbers dramatically declined. The rabbit is now so much part of the circle of life regarding prey species for many raptors and carnivores that its extinction would rapidly alter the balance of nature. Also the landscape would be altered dramatically to the detriment of certain species of wild flowers and plants that rely on close-cropped downland to survive and this in turn would affect the butterfly world.

As the road began to rise once again winding its way through to the district of Rogart and eventually home via Loch Fleet, the kestrel, disturbed by the buzzard, flew off towards the rough grassland on the other side of the river. He suddenly checked and hovered. With the late afternoon sun glinting on his chestnut back and grey head and his grey black banded tail fanned out and pointing down for stability, he appeared as a last fitting tribute to herald the end of 'raptor alley'.

Chapter 10

SWALLOWS SURVIVAL

Nobody would believe it was just past midsummers day. With the last few weeks temperatures in the mid teens and little sun, today was as dreche, dull and misty as ever. But everyday has a silver lining and so it was today. I had taken my dog, Bracken, on one of her scheduled walks to the local woodland that lined a peaceful loch. Half way through her constitutional she was disturbed by the continued barking of what she at first thought was a fellow dog. Realising it was not canine she became agitated. The sound had been coming from half way up the slopes of Migdale Rock and after reassuring her I proceeded to investigate. The barking had subsided to a certain extent, which made it more difficult to pin-point, but suddenly I caught a slight movement between the twisted and knarled branches of the Scots pine trees in the foreground. The foxy red form of a roe deer was suddenly apparent as it foraged amongst the rocks and scattered bushes on the lower slopes of the cliff face. As this smallest of our native deer raised its head to sniff for danger I could see the short sharp antlers protruding from his head, which he threw further back to bark twice at any rival males which may have been close-by, before returning to browse on an accessible tree shoot. How beautiful he was, dressed in his sleek summer coat with black nose and white chin patch glistening with dew from the damp foliage and his large furry ears twitching on either side of his three pointed pearl based antlers. This is the beginning of the rutting or mating season and although usually a quiet and secretive animal the males during this period are particularly vocal and therefore vulnerable. Suddenly he caught our scent on the swirling mist and disappeared into more dense undergrowth.

The loch was like a millpond where every small ripple created by the last of the mayflies on the waters surface, was magnified a hundred times. The air was still and only nature's sounds invaded the silence - male chaffinches exuberant flourish of notes, hooded crows "kraaring" from a distant perch and the high pitched "twi-wi-wi-wee" of an excitable common sandpiper at the waters edge. Hidden amongst the multitude of bird song was a soft gentle wailing cry that appeared to come from the direction of the loch. Effortlessly gliding through the still waters was not one but six red-throated divers, apparently enjoying each other's company. The lead bird was the vocal one but this half-hearted attempt at a territorial display led me to believe that they were immature birds and not yet of breeding age. This very unusual behaviour persisted on further visits reinforcing my theory.

After our walk we returned home for the usual coffee and biscuits, me a coffee, her a biscuit. After this treat she settled down on her bean-bed and I resumed work. One of my usual daily chores is to collect firewood from the ample supply stored in the barn. On entering the half-stable door I was confronted by the pair of resident breeding swallows flitting around in apparent disarray and chittering in alarm before disappearing through the hole in the gable end that I had enlarged the previous year. Being concerned about their disturbed state I approached their nesting area to discover to my horror their nest, lying on the bare floor fully twenty feet below its original position. Swallows have nested in the barn every single year during our occupation and usually rear two broods before migrating to South Africa for the winter months. This year, very unusually after some minor repairs, they had re-used the previous years' nest. This was situated high on the apex of a roof truss, which was completely safe from any predators like our cats. Unfortunately the dried mud and straw of the old construction was beginning to lose some of its adhesion to the wooden truss but the new repairs had appeared to be holding it in position. Apparently my optimism was misplaced as the remains of the nest, with one youngster still in place was lying at my feet. I quickly looked around to find one ball of black feathers lying motionless on the bare boarded floor and one more fortunate youngster cradled amongst some split bales of hay. Fearing the worst I picked them up and to my amazement none appeared any the worst for their ordeal. They all needed about a further week in the nest before becoming fully fledged so drastic action had to be taken. I carefully placed them in a straw lined box and contemplated the problem. I could not reach the apex of the roof where the nest had been attached, even with my extending ladders, and any alternative site was ruled out either by lack of a suitable position where the parents would easily find the relocated youngsters or the difficulty in safely securing the battered nest. The only sensible alternative was to secure it to a cross beam which stretched from one side of the barn to the other directly beneath the original site, be it ten feet away but adjacent to the gable entrance hole. The repair was comparatively simple. Using a piece of rabbit wire netting I shaped it into a cup in which I placed the semi-circular construction and built up the rest of the cup using small pieces of hay and dried moss to form a regular shaped nest. I then secured the nest to the beam using metal staples through the rabbit netting. Surveying my handy work I then realised how vulnerable the new site was to the chief predators in our garden, our cats. As I was wrapping some further wire netting around each end of the beam to prevent the cats from climbing up I felt I was being watched. I turned around and there peering out from the gloom of a darkened corner was Oliver, our grey and white male cat, purring contentedly with his front feet tucked underneath him looking as if butter wouldn't melt in his mouth. He had obviously been intently watching all the proceedings with interest. Negotiate that I said confidently! Having completed all the construction work I carefully placed the fledglings in the makeshift nest. Immediately the more advanced one promptly half flew, half fell, out of the nest to crash land into the soft hay below. This happened two or three times until finally I placed one of his siblings on top of him or her and quickly scurried down the ladder to avoid further disturbance. With the three young swallows secured and settled in the nest I retired to the house to allow things to settle down. After about an hour I crept back into the barn whilst the parents were away hunting for insects to feed the youngsters and hid in a darkened corner to await their return. Within ten minutes both parents had arrived through the gable entrance hole, perched on the beam and fed their voracious brood. The frantic proceedings hadn't impressed Oliver one little bit, he couldn't understand what all the fuss was about and had promptly fallen asleep. A week later the youngsters had fledged and were joining their parents in aerial displays over the garden. A great success all round I thought.

Chapter 11

SEALED WITH A SNARL

GREY SEAL AND PUP

The north coast of Sutherland has much in common with the coastline of Cornwall. Both have high cliffs that are pounded by high seas creating significant erosion to induce unusual rock formations and small inaccessible sandy bays. But this is where the similarity ends as the inhospitable hinterland of Sutherland is in stark contrast to the lush green vegetation of Cornwall. One of my favourite places to visit on the north coast at any time of the year is the small village of Tongue which is situated on the Kyle of the same name and overlooked by the "Queen of Scottish mountains" Ben Loyal.

My journey began on a bright, relatively mild day around the middle of October, when walking the hills is out of bounds (because of red deer stalking) and the numbers of migrating waders and wildfowl are beginning to build up. From late September the skeins of greylag geese flying over my garden from their breeding grounds in the north to their wintering grounds further south have increased in number as the weeks have gone by. Even on a clear night their honking can be heard piercing the still air as they navigate the glistening waters of the Kyle of Sutherland and the Inner Dornoch Firth beyond. The greylag is Britain's only native goose but a gradual decline has reduced the population to around 700 to 800 pairs. These numbers are insignificant compared with the 90,000 plus that winter here, mainly from Iceland. The other bird sound of autumn over the garden is the loud trumpeting "whoop" as small family groups of whooper swans make their way to Loch Eye, an inland refuge in Ross-shire, from their breeding grounds also in Iceland. Unlike the native mute swan the whooper is generally noisy, especially in flight and what a sight they make as they fly overhead. This very large white bird with its neck held out straight emits intermittent wild whoops as it disappears into the distance. About 7,000 to 9,000 winter in Britain with Scotland holding a large amount of the population. But unlike the geese, whoopers move extensively around the country and are widely dispersed with many family parties and small groups occupying the more remote lochs. A truly wild swan.

With the golden brown leaves of sleepy trees fluttering down around the Land Rover I headed out through my village to follow the River Shin northwards. As I entered the small town of Lairg I glanced along the narrow head of Loch Shin towards the hydro-electric dam and power station, but nothing stirred apart from the occasional circular ripples from rising fish. It was a different story this summer, when not one but three individual black-throated divers graced me with their presence on this small stretch of water, which runs parallel with the main road and very close to civilisation. The majestic beauty of these birds can only be fully appreciated at close quarters and the nearest specimen filled the binocular frame totally. The adult breeding plumage of all birds are beautiful in their own way but the black-throats in my opinion defy imagination. Perhaps I am biased because it is one of my true favourites. Although basically black and white it is the striking patterns that appear unreal. The pale grey velvet head is highlighted by a jet-black throat, which is bordered by a black and white stripped neck that extends down to the breast like running mascara. A black and white chequered back completes the picture, apart from the piercing red eye, which captures with a subtle glint its true wild character.

Just outside Lairg there is a main junction with one road leading to the north-west but I am headed due north into what can only be described as a mini flow country. "Flow country" is a term used in conservation circles for a tree-less area of sphagnum moss covered bog interspersed by lochs, lochans and dubh lochans (small pools). I was once engaged to conduct an environmental bird survey for a forestry company on an area of land adjoining this particular road but despite my reservations on the validity of any further conifer plantations, the planting went ahead. I often think that these surveys are just a paper exercise to satisfy Government legislation. Fortunately the importance of these marshy areas has been realised and the need for blanket forestry reduced which should enable divers, greenshank, redshank and dunlin, along with the common scoter and wigeon to breed in peace.

Once past the isolated outpost of Crask Inn the road left the marshland behind to follow the River Vagastie to the village of Altnaharra. All along the course of the river small fragmented areas of birch, rowan, alder and very old oak grew in contrast to desolate heather and deer grass hillsides. This oasis was full of blackbirds, redwings and mistle thrushes on migration from Scandinavia, gorging themselves on the remaining berries and insects hidden under the leaf litter, before moving further south as winter approached. Above the strath (river valley) towered the sprawling mass of Ben Klibreck whose long heathery slopes rise to over 3,000 feet above the surrounding moorland. Dotterel are said to breed amongst the plant rich tundra that forms the flat summit plateau. These birds are unique in so much that it is the male who unusually has the duller plumage, incubates the eggs and undertakes almost all the parental duties after hatching.

As I drove into the hamlet of Altnaharra the activity within the very small community was strikingly obvious. A school playground full of small children bussed in from miles around created a noise not synonymous with the isolated surroundings and a busy hotel car park was full of guests leaving for excursions into the hills to stalk red deer. The same activity applied to the summer but with salmon fishing substituting for deer stalking and with the notoriety of often being mentioned on the TV national weather forecast regarding temperature and conditions in the far north, this isolated community was doing very nicely thank you.

I crossed the bridge over the River Mudale, which flowed into the picturesque Loch Naver and was confronted by the great northern cross-roads. Two large stone pillars stood guard over the road north to Tongue and to the east the road wound along Loch Naver to Bettyhill, but the road I had decided to take was single tracked and heralded with the sign "Not Suitable for Caravans". An ominous start!

Once on the road I could see why caravans would be a hazard. The road itself was very narrow with small passing places, which would make manoeuvring past some of the larger caravans virtually impossible. The first mile or so was pretty uneventful, apart from negotiating around the wandering sheep from the neighbouring farm that nestled down by the river surrounded by green fields. An island amongst the vast landscape of brown heather and deer grass. Suddenly everything changed and I was surrounded by red deer stags grazing with the sheep or lying in the heather casually chewing the cud right next to the road. Most were fairly young stags although there were a few more mature ones but they were just too small for the trophy hunters to care about. Even at this young age it seemed as though they knew that being near to the road and civilisation was the safest place to be at this time of year, although when I stopped the vehicle for a longer look they became decidedly uneasy. The in-built fear of Land Rovers and the hunting fraternity they usually contain had been etched in their minds long ago, when they witnessed members of the herd disappearing when these vehicles were in the vicinity. Unfortunately they could not know that I meant them no harm and gradually they moved further away.

After the road had dissected a small conifer plantation it emerged at the head of Loch Meadie, a very long narrow stretch of water bedecked with a number of small islands and surrounded by a brown carpet of heather stretching as far as the eye could see. I was just about to continue when two large white shapes came into view from behind a small promontory and swam further into a patch of water reeds. They could only be a couple of wild whooper swans who had stopped off on their way south from their northern breeding range. From this distance the yellow angular patch on the black bill was clearly visible. These swans ooze wildness and this, coupled with their chosen extremely remote habitat, is in complete contrast to the attitude and demeanour of the decorative, relatively urbanised familiar mute swan. When not feeding their long necks are always stretched high to keep an eye out for potential danger as shown by their uneasiness at any intrusion.

The whooper swans had been a bonus in this otherwise desolate but beautiful landscape. Desolation in this sense is a human trait, for I do not think the number of red deer I saw would agree. Around every bend on the twisting road small groups of hinds either rose from the heather, skipped across in front of the Land Rover or disappeared behind the many rough grass covered knolls. But the classic sight was left to the end. As I approached the final stretch of the level part of the road, before it plunged steeply from three hundred feet to sea level, there standing on a heather strewn mound was a magnificent eight pointer (antlers) prime stag, surveying the river and surrounding hills way below in Strathmore as if he was king of all he indeed surveyed.

The river meandered through a green swathe of rough pasture that was cropped by cattle, sheep and stalking ponies whose diet was now supplemented by bales of hay and straw. With the steep descent behind me I continued until I came across an old Pictish tower that was constructed many years ago as a defensive position for the inhabitants of the glen. Dun Dornaigil broch has been carefully preserved and although you cannot enter it is none the less very impressive, but not as impressive as the mighty Ben Hope that towers above the road in two crag-lined tiers to just over 3,000 feet. Just beyond the broch a small parking area had been constructed with a signpost "Ben Hope way up" placed in a prominent position. I couldn't help thinking, as I watched a pair of well equipped climbers following the well defined path that wound its way up and along the banks of the cascading mountain stream, that the sign belittles this grand mountain and significantly more, the most northerly Munro. (A Munro is a Scottish mountain exceeding 3,000 feet in height and is attributed to Sir Hugh Munro, who in 1891 published his meticulous records listing all of them arranged in districts and in descending order of altitude, including any subsidiary tops not considered separate mountains). Young readers must excuse my reference to the heights of Scottish mountains in feet as opposed to metres. On current ordnance survey maps all altitudes are indicated in metres to satisfy Brussels and the EEC but I feel that Ben Hope's impressive 3,040 feet has been degraded to a meagre 927 metres and that does not have quite the same ring to it.

Driving along the narrow road was a sheer delight, with on one side the lower slopes of the Ben bedecked with dwarf birch and rowan and on the other the start of Loch Hope sparkling in the mid-day sun. Along the initial part of the lochside the road wound its way through a narrow corridor of deciduous woodland where the resident tits and chaffinches were being serenaded by winter robins proclaiming their territories. As the loch began to narrow towards its exit into Loch Eriboll and eventually the open sea, the landscape changed back to the familiar moorland scene but still the strip of arable land adjoining the lochside clung on to produce a meagre existence for the local crofters. This caravan free road eventually ended at the tiny hamlet of Hope, which only consisted of about half a dozen houses. As I was about to turn right onto the laughingly called main road to Tongue, I glanced back from where I had just come from and instantly wished I had brought my camera. There in the foreground was a well kept croft house with off-white harled walls and slate roof nestling in a hollow next to the free flowing river that meandered from the loch to the sea. A scattering of birch and willow broke up the surrounding undulated rough grassland with in the background the mass of Ben Hope towering over the shimmering silvery waters of the loch. A classic photograph suitable to adorn any Scottish calendar.

The view as I began to descend towards Tongue was breathtaking compared to the desolate moorland I had just crossed from the junction at Hope. The scene was dominated by Ben Loyal, whose four gracefully sculptured and linked granite tops rose abruptly from the moorland floor with the still waters of Lochan Dherue lying beneath her feet. From this distance her stature appears immense but her highest peak barely tops 2,500 feet. (Why are mountains always referred to in the feminine gender?) In the foreground the causeway over the Kyle of Tongue was small by comparison although it added a sense of interest to the whole picture. Created to save the long but picturesque journey around the southern end of the Kyle, this man-made structure of rock and tarmac has produced feeding areas for a wide variety of birds at low tide.

This was also the time to watch common seals, flippers pointing skywards basking on the huge sandbanks that stretch virtually across the entire Kyle. But first I am off to Talmine, a small village on the way to the uninhabited north coast of high cliffs and tempestuous seas. So I turned left before crossing over the causeway to follow the narrow road past the most scenically positioned graveyard in the country. It may not mean much to the inhabitants but to relatives and others who tend the graves the view up the Kyle to Ben Loyal is unsurpassable, even though many Highland cemeteries are positioned in places of outstanding beauty. A mixture of old croft houses, refurbished ones and new bungalows lined the road-side into Talmine where the decision had to be made to take the high road past the combined post office and village store or the lower road to the beach. I took the low road and stopped next to the shell of a boat long since abandoned on the beach, whose rotting timbers had played host to numerous wood boring insects and was covered in fungus and bleached almost white by the sun and sea spray. A small group of male and female eider duck floated leisurely around the tranquil sheltered bay but there were others taking advantage of the calm waters. Further out a black-throated diver in winter plumage continued to dive until at last successful settled on the surface to preen. The birds' striking summer garb disappears totally in winter to reveal a rather drab dark grey head and back that merges into a white neck and breast. Like most winter plumages, dull but still great to see. As were the razorbills and guillemots, whose black and white forms could just be made out on the edge of the more turbulent water as the tide began to turn.

A short incline led me to the pier which was basically a concrete wall stretched between the mainland and a small island lying thirty yards off-shore. This was where last summer I saw my first otter in this area. I was sitting in the Land Rover casually watching the world go by and a small group of eiders diving for molluscs when my attention was drawn to a movement amongst the rocks just below my position. Suddenly the creature appeared, jumped onto a large flat boulder and began crunching its way through a large crab. I could then clearly see it was an otter and judging by the size, heavy head and thick neck, a male or dog otter. Females appear more delicate and gentile and are slightly smaller. After having his fill he picked his way through the seaweed covered rocks to emerge on a small shingle beach left exposed by the tide. He then slid silently into the water to re-emerge amongst the small flotilla of boats anchored just off-shore tucking into a pale coloured butterfish, which disappeared in minutes. Not yet satisfied he swam towards the small island that supported one end of the concrete pier creating a wide 'v' shaped wake. He continued to forage amongst the rocks for anything edible before he disappeared around the other side of the island. I didn't see him again. Typical otter behaviour!

Although the tramaced road ended at the pier, a small track gauged out of the rock and heather ran parallel to the coastline for a couple of hundred yards before petering out at a grass covered parking area overlooking a sandy beach. Just passable in a normal car, the Land Rover made easy progress over the pot-holed stone covered surface. During the summer months white rumped wheatears and dapper little pied wagtails flit between the rough grassland and rocky outcrops that border the track looking for insects to catch for their new broods. But at this time of year most have departed apart from a few stragglers and it was one of these that caught my eye a couple of autumns ago. One late, relatively warm October day as I was having my lunch at the parking area a brightly coloured wheatear was searching between the rocks for the last remaining insects. Compared to the familiar British species, it was larger with longer legs and the boldness of its plumage confirmed it was a member of the Greenland sub-species on migration. A great find.

I parked facing the sea as the Land Rovers virtually straight windscreen reduces the distortion to a minimum. A quick scan with the binoculars before lunch revealed all that I was expecting to see. Continuing fly-pasts of cormorants and shags, diving winter plumaged guillemots and razorbills, probing oystercatchers and curlews, eiders riding the waves and the most spectacular a small flotilla of long-tailed ducks. The scenic view from my position was equally spectacular. The small silvery sandy bay in front of me gave rise to a rocky island backdrop. About a mile off-shore lie Rabbit Islands, three large chunks of rock of a hundred and fifty feet or so, one with a visible natural arch created by the continual erosion of the sandstone cliffs by the pounding of ferocious seas. It is not known at what date rabbits were first introduced into Sutherland but they were established on the Islands by 1793. Beyond Rabbit Islands is the larger island of Eilean nan Ron whose highest point is over two hundred feet and its two claims to fame are both connected with wildlife. There are only two places in Sutherland where the Atlantic grey seals are known to breed, one is among the caves on the islands' north shore and the other, again around caves, near Freisgill on Whiten Head. The other claim is that the island is the main centre in the north for wintering flocks of barnacle geese from their breeding grounds in Greenland, but unless you have use of a boat both these phenomenons are inaccessible.

After satisfying my appetite I decided to walk firstly along the short stretch of beach that the increasingly rising tide would soon cover and then up and over the heather clad cliff top along the coastal fringe. A large rocky area dominated the north side of the beach and to a lesser extent on the other, creating a small cove. One of the more unusual aspects of this particular part of the coastline is how the upper reaches of the beach have been formed. Not of sand but slabs of rock in assorted shapes and sizes about half an inch thick encrusted with veins of mica sparkling like precious jewels. These have broken away from the surrounding rock faces and have been washed smooth by the waves and tides for many years. In geological terms the flaggy or slab formation of sandstone found in this area is characteristic of rocks of the Moine Series of metamorphosed sediments known as Moinian. These rocks make up by far the greatest part of Sutherland and were first formed about 750 million years ago.

A large rocky area dominated the northern side of the beach and I soon discovered the tell-tale tracks of an otter in the wet sand as it emerged from the sea to begin its search for food. I tracked it first to the rocks themselves and then to where they re-appeared next to a rock pool left by the previous receding tide. This deep pool was lined with pink coral weed and contained several species of red, brown and green seaweed, which was itself being grazed upon by common limpets. These pools, usually edged by barnacles, provide shelter for small fish, prawns, anemones and crabs, which make for a tasty snack for a scavenging otter. As I was scrambling over the rocks trying to track the movements of this elusive creature I came across a white-coated seal pup lying on a small sandy beach that was exposed on one side to the open sea. I could only assume that either its mother had gone to fish for her supper or my approach had frightened her away. It appeared to be in good health and well fed but where it was positioned the large waves, that were accompanying the incoming tide, were crashing over the rocks and the pup was in danger of being washed into the sea. Until this pup had shed its white coat and become more buoyant it would have drowned, so I decided to take a hand and move it further up the beach. This was easier said than done, as my good intentions were obviously not appreciated. After several approaches, where the only gratitude I received was a snarl and a biting lunge, I eventually managed to grab its back flippers and drag it carefully over the sand and onto a small gravel bank. This bank was just high enough to protect the pup from the worst of the turbulent waves. Having done my good dead for the day I beat a hasty retreat in case its mother wanted to return to feed the little mite whose large dark eyes followed my every move. Usually grey seals breed in colonies but for some unknown reason this ones mother wanted or was forced to be on her own. An Atlantic grey seal cow bears only one pup that feeds on her rich milk for three weeks in which time it triples its birth weight. After this time it sheds its long creamy white baby coat to become pale grey and at two months old is ready to go to sea.

I continued walking northwards along a narrow sheep track which cut through the brittle heather stems to emerge at the side of a large burn. The crystal clear waters tumbled over several large boulders forming mini-waterfalls before disappearing down the rest of the cliff face and into the sea. I carefully traversed the burn by using the boulders as stepping-stones before following a further sheep track, which snaked its way towards a large hill that dominated the surrounding undulating terrain. Once negotiated I settled down, precariously close to the cliff edge, with an uninterrupted view along the shore to the furthest point and across to two small islands that were no bigger than a couple of large rocks.

Fortunately I had decided to carry my telescope and tripod with me, for although cumbersome it is essential for sea watching. Nestling behind a rock for protection from the stiff breeze that had begun to blow, I scanned the endless amount of water before me. With the naked eye I had already spotted several sparkling white plumaged birds dotted around, conspicuous against the dark blue background of the sea. At first I thought they were just gulls but on reflection they did appear on the small side, even from this distance. As I began to focus my telescope on one of these subjects it dived. Obviously not a gull! It re-surfaced a little further out to reveal the mystery - a black guillemot in winter plumage. This bird's (whose local name is 'tystie') summer plumage is a completely black body except for white wing patches, whereas at this time of year the upper parts of its body are barred black and white with the head and underparts mainly white. A total reversal from one season to another.

Shags and their cousins, the cormorants, continued to fly low over the water between the islands with the occasional bird perched on a rock with wings held out to dry in characteristic posture. Looking northwards and further out to sea the sky was full of large birds, some brilliant white, some plain brown and others a combination of both. From their distinctive shape I could tell they were gannets, ranging from immature first year birds through to fourth year adults and probably from the breeding colonies of Sula Sgeir or Sule Stack far off the north coast. There is a wide dispersal of these birds through northern European waters throughout the autumn with some continuing a gradual southward movement as far as the Mediterranean. Some of the gannets were plunging vertically into the sea in spectacular fashion after spotting a shoal of fish while others were just sailing around on their massive six foot wingspan.

Panning back along the coastline I suddenly saw a movement in the corner of the telescope's lens but by the time I had adjusted and focused, it had disappeared beneath the waves. So I waited and waited and waited, nothing! I returned to my binoculars and with the greater field of view found it preening on the surface of the water. The telescope once again revealed all - obviously a diver of some sort in its usual dull winter plumage, but which one? Large bulky form, steep forehead and heavy bill carried horizontally, it had to be a great northern. Almost all these species of bird seen off British coasts are winter visitors only, for their main breeding range is in North America where they are known by the seemingly disrespectful name of the 'common loon'. There are also smaller populations in Iceland and Greenland where presumably our visitors come from.

On my last trip to the Isle of Skye, around the middle of May, I was fortunate enough and amazed to find a great northern in every bay I visited along the northern coastline of the Sleat peninsular. With the majestic snow capped Cuillin mountain range as a backdrop and the rare sight of a great northern diver in its splendid summer plumage, what could be better. One was so close I could even make out the patterned neck patches but the wailing, eerie, territorial call that echoes across the lonely waters of its breeding grounds was unfortunately not to be heard. I have only experienced this phenomenon on film, never in the flesh so to speak.

As the day wore on the late afternoon began to feel a bit chilly so I retraced my steps along the steep tracks, over the burn and gave the seal pup a wide berth before arriving back at the Land Rover. Having made my way back along the track to the pier and then along the road through Talmine, I turned left at the junction to cross the causeway to Tongue. I stopped on the small steel bridge that allows the water to ebb and flow with the tide to admire a large group of eiders sitting amongst the rocks above the high water mark, most of whom had their heads tucked under their wings. The best time to stop in either of the two parking spots along the causeway is at low tide where the exposed seaweed covered rocks are a magnet to hungry birds. Curlew, redshank, dunlin, oystercatcher and ringed plover all scurry about probing and searching for worms, molluscs and shell fish during the short period when the rocks remain uncovered. While wigeon, teal and mallard dabble at the waters edge watched over by that weary of sentries, the grey heron.

It was on this causeway last summer when I again did my good deed that was appreciated by all and sundry. This time I was driving away from Tongue when I noticed something on the road in front of me. I slowed down and was amazed to find my vehicle confronted by a very perturbed male shelduck running around like a headless chicken. Before I had time to think about what was happening, his female accompanied by ten small humbug striped chicks ran towards him in an equally panic-stricken state. They had obviously emerged from the seaward side of the Kyle and had found themselves on the road, which was at that point lined by a two foot wall. Although the adults could fly over this obstacle the youngsters were trapped with the possibility of being run over. There was only one thing I could do. As there was nothing coming in either direction, I turned my head lights and hazard warning lights on and began to shepherd the family towards the first gap in the wall, which was at the entrance to the first parking area about thirty yards further on. Using the Land Rover as a mechanical sheepdog and by weaving all over the road I managed to keep them moving in the right direction. I then realised that there were cars coming towards me but realising the situation they had slowed down and finally stopped just before the opening in the wall. I jumped out of the Land Rover and coerced the entire family through the entrance and to the freedom of the mud flats. As I turned a crescendo of applause greeted me from the owners of the cars that had stopped in convoy in both directions. I politely bowed, thanked them and proceeded on my way smiling contentedly.

Tongue is a green and well-wooded village, an oasis among the barren peat bog and heather moorland associated with this most northerly landscape. This contrast was fully appreciated as I stood on the summit plateau of Brae Kirkiboll on my way out of the village on the road back to Altnaharra. I have often said to visitors that in the Highlands there is an incredible view around every corner and this was no exception. North - from the 14th century Varrick Castle (although only a few walls remain) perched on a prominent hill overlooking the Kyle of Tongue to the open sea, west - over the desolate heather moorland to the rounded slopes of Ben Hope and finally south - along the fertile valley of the Kinloch River overlooked by the picturesque Ben Loyal.

On reflection it had been a good day and an interesting one and as the sun began to sink lower in the sky I turned the Land Rover towards home.

Chapter 12

EMBO - A PLACE FOR BIRDS!

RINGED PLOVER

In the summer months the coastal area of south-east Sutherland is best known for its championship links golf courses, extensive near deserted golden sands and soft rolling countryside. When the tourists have departed and autumn starts to change to winter, nature begins its forced state of limbo until the full flood of spring. The only places where this is not apparent are the estuaries and coastal margins that become swollen with wintering wildfowl, waders and passage migrants from more northerly latitudes.

One of the best places to observe the ever-increasing numbers is Loch Fleet, a natural tidal basin situated between the county towns of Dornoch and Golspie, the capital town and seat of the Duke of Sutherland at nearby Dunrobin Castle. But the piece de resistance lies about one mile south of the Fleet. To anyone who knows east Sutherland the name Embo probably signifies the "Grannie's Heilan Hame" caravan site with row upon row of static caravans lined up adjacent to the beach accompanied by hoards of tourers during the summer season. At this time of year though it becomes a place for birds.

One of the most interesting ways to get to Embo from my home is via the Loch Bhudie moorland road, along the southern flanks of Loch Fleet followed by a small diversion off the main route that leads to Dornoch. During the spring and summer months the single track road which winds its way through heather and bracken covered moorland to Loch Fleet is alive with bird song. Willow warblers, redpolls, great and blue tits sing from a prominent perch in the sparse willow and birch scrub, wrens and stonechats battle for supremacy amongst the heather and bracken stems, curlews call as they descend and disappear into the dense older heather and buzzards 'kiew' as they soar on the thermals. But on this November day silence reigned.

After having an enjoyable but disappointing drive my luck began to change and how! As I began the steady but gradual descent from the high moors to the estuary, there in the distance sitting on a grassy knoll, was a large bird silhouetted against the sky. Due to its position I could not see any colour variations and therefore assumed it was a buzzard. I stopped the Land Rover and immediately the big bird took off, dropping below the skyline and heading along the road straight for me. I grabbed my binoculars and fell out of the door all in one movement, for I had realised that it was a golden eagle and it was very unusually heading in my direction. At this point, as if reading my thoughts, the bird veered to its right and headed for the distant hills. This was an immature eagle and judging by the amount and intensity of white markings on the underside of its wings and tail it must have been one of this years brood looking to establish its own territory. With a few flaps of its massive wings interspersed with long glides this magnificent bird had negotiated the high voltage electric cables between the intruding steel pylons and was disappearing behind the nearest heather and bracken covered hill. I wished it luck; with the end of time of plenty fast approaching many juvenile eagles do not survive their first Highland winter because of their lack of ability and experience to find sufficient food to sustain them.

This was indeed a great start and as I continued to descend from the high moors through the now tree lined road of alder, birch and rowan to the head of Loch Fleet, I wondered what other treats the day would hold. The small single-track road, which skirts the southern side of Loch Fleet, is ideal for bird watching for its many passing places make it easy to stop and use the vehicle as a hide. The resident wildfowl and wader numbers are swollen by many migrants making their way south to escape the harsh northern winters. Loch Fleet being the most northerly inlet on the east coast of Scotland is the first stopping off place for wigeon, mallard, teal, greylag geese and many more wildfowl from their breeding quarters in northern Europe, Scandinavia and the Arctic tundra.

The most numerous duck on the loch is the wigeon, sometimes numbering in their thousands and they are unusual among duck in that they will often graze on grass and mudflat plants like geese. At this time of year the flocks are in their duller winter plumage but the drake is still a handsome specimen with his chestnut head adorned with a pale cream crown. The British breeding birds, about 300-400 pairs, are confined to Scotland and northern England and this number has built up over the years since the first nest was discovered in Sutherland in 1834.

Teal are Britain's smallest duck and because they are the wildfowlers favourite quarry they are very wary and took flight as soon as I stopped to get a closer look. They are one of my favourites too, but obviously not for the same reason, the male with his dark chestnut head, green eye-patch and yellow under-tail feathers must make it one of the most attractive of our ducks.

At this time of year the most obvious duck, not only on the loch but also all around our coasts must be the barge-like eider. Being the largest and most numerous European sea duck coupled with the breeding males striking black and white plumage, he is hard to miss. It takes up to four years to reach full plumage and from July onwards until after their moult, the adult and young males share an eclipse plumage consisting of various degrees of black and white contrasting with the plain dull brown of the females. To me the eiders seem to epitomize the way of life in the Highlands, never appearing to rush even when feeding and often floating around aimlessly quite content and at peace with their own little world.

Approaching the ruin of Skelbo Castle, where fulmars and jackdaws share a communal nesting site, a small pull-in and picnic site has been constructed overlooking a rocky spit where a small burn runs under the road and into the loch. Most people stop here and I'm no exception. As the burn is fresh water many birds congregate at the waters edge to preen their feathers to keep them in pristine condition. Sea birds often seek out fresh water to bathe the same way that human's shower after a swim in the sea, to remove salt. The vast majority of birds actually bathing were gulls, mainly common but a few black-headed and greater black-backed. Individual oyster catchers, redshanks and curlews were also getting in on the act, having separated from the main flocks that were resting nearby with their heads tucked into their wings and standing on one leg. Also dabbling at the waters edge and sifting through the weed-strewn gravel were small groups of wigeon, teal and mallard. As an added bonus a male red-breasted merganser was fishing off the point. This colourful bird is a saw-billed duck equipped with fine serrations on its bill for gripping wet slippery fish. This male was in full plumage after two months of the eclipse stage when he resembles the female apart from his more pronounced white wing patch. This very distinctive bird with his dark green head sporting an untidy double crest, blood red bill, white collar and chestnut breast is easily recognisable. Along with his cousin, the goosander, both these species are persecuted by water bailiffs who, because they are excluded from the "Wild Bird Protection Act in Scotland", can shoot them because of their alleged effect on the numbers of young salmon and trout. A tragic end to the only two species of sawbill duck that breed in the British Isles.

Looking east from my vantage point I could see the 80ft deep exit channel at Littleferry and the rough sea beyond. Although it was a bright sunny day with blue skies and white fluffy clouds, a strong south easterly wind was blowing which had the effect of reducing the temperature and increasing the size of the white capped waves on the open sea.

Leaving Loch Fleet behind it is but a few miles to the small village of Embo. Like many villages along the north-east coast it once had a fine fishing tradition, but alas no more. Once past the village outskirts, which are lined with newly constructed tiny terraced cottages in keeping with the traditional low gable style of 1820 when the village was established, the caravan site looms up in all its glory. I am heading for the grassy bank overlooking a small rocky outcrop, which breaks up the monotony of the seemingly endless sandy beach at the far end of the site. I parked my Land Rover side-on to the sea so that if necessary I could use the telescope from within the vehicle as the strong penetrating south-east wind was extremely cold, reducing the eyes to tears within minutes. Because of the state of the tide many of the furthest boulders had disappeared but their presence was betrayed by the resulting white water fury created by the endless contest between the sea and the intruding rock. A cursory glance at the nearest rocks revealed nothing until a slight movement caught my eye. Standing there on the edge of a small pool, created by erosion on the soft sandstone, was a small flock of redshank accompanied by a few turnstones, all with their beaks tucked into their wings waiting for the tide to turn. They had been virtually invisible with their dull winter plumage blending in with the dappled rocks. Resting waders are a bit like children; they find it impossible to keep still and are continually fidgeting due to their close proximity to each other. It was during one of these bouts of infighting that I realised that tucked in amongst the turnstones were a few of their winter associates - purple sandpipers. Both these birds are winter visitors to our coastal areas, the turnstone from its breeding grounds in the Arctic (although some non-breeders spend the summer on the north-east coast of Scotland) and the purple sandpiper from northern Scandinavia and Iceland. They also prefer the same feeding habitat of a rocky shoreline where the orange-legged turnstone can literally turn over small stones and seaweed exposed at low tide in search of sand hoppers and other small shore life. The purple sandpiper, which gets its name from the purple gloss of its upper parts in summer plumage, feeds on shellfish found in amongst the same seaweed covered rocks. Further along the shoreline several other waders began to appear as if on cue from behind larger rock formations. There were a few oyster catchers, a couple of curlew and all of a sudden a flock of small waders consisting of ringed plover and dunlin, descended in a grey whirling cloud to where the golden sand joined the encroaching spume.

But the most interesting aspect of Embo at this time of year is sea watching. With the sea quite rough this posed its own problems because no sooner had I discovered something it disappeared behind the next wave. But some birds are easily seen no matter what the weather. I am of course talking about the eider duck whose striking black and white plumage of the males makes it unmistakable. There were several groups of males and females bobbing around like corks about thirty yards off-shore being kept company by the much smaller long-tailed duck. Sea ducks always amaze me by their total indifference to the wildness of their environment. The fifteen foot swell seemed to make no difference at all, they continued to dive for shellfish or just rode the waves seemingly enjoying the enforced ride on natures big dipper. The long-tailed duck is one of the worlds' most northerly breeding species spanning the entire northern

138

hemisphere, from the northern coasts of Europe to North America and extending into Greenland and Iceland. It feeds on a variety of molluscs and crustaceans diving to nearly 60m to reach annelid worms. This delightful little brown and white duck (predominantly white in winter and brown in summer) is, apart from the pintail, the only other duck with a long tail in northern Europe. Along with the red-breasted mergansers, cormorants and gulls, these birds are regular features of the Embo landscape.

Just beyond where the sea was crashing against the exposed rocks, creating a ten foot high white water cascade, were three species who although less numerous are regular visitors to our coastal waters at this time of year. Continually diving as the mountainous waves approached was a single slavonian grebe and two red-throated divers in their drab winter plumage. Although the grebe is somewhat smaller than the diver both are predominantly white with dark grey markings from the crown down the back of the neck to the back. Both species nest on small lochs but the diver prefers the more remote hill lochans and is much more numerous and widespread. The first breeding pair of slavonian grebes was seen in Scotland in 1908 and since that time there are now only about 60 pairs established on shallow freshwater lochs in Inverness-shire. The third species, although further out, was in less turbulent waters and with the aid of the telescope was easily identified. This large diver shaped black and white bird with its heavy bill and brilliant white underparts gleaming in the sunlight as it rolled over to preen itself was unmistakable. The bulky form of the great northern diver is distinctive at any time of the year, but more especially in May on the west Highland coast in full breeding plumage, when making its way to its arctic breeding grounds. This particular diver was complimented by a continual fly-past of juvenile gannets emerging from the distant sea mist. Most of these gannets were the spangled brown first year birds with the occasional appearance of a gleaming white adult, for it takes four years to reach mature plumage. The immature birds having been bred at the nearest colony on Sule Stack about 50 miles off the north coast were on their way to winter off West Africa.

Suddenly my attention was drawn to the sound of rapidly beating wings and alarm calls from the roosting waders and gulls. There flying along the beach towards me was the reason, the daunting shape of the pirates of the north seas - skuas. Throughout October and November arctic and great skua's occasionally pass down our eastern coast on the way to their wintering quarters in the southern Atlantic, but these three birds appeared slightly different. They had the slimmer, tern like shape of the arctic but appeared slightly larger. It wasn't until they were level with me that I realised with great excitement that one was an adult pale plumaged pomarine skua, with its characteristic elongated tail shape formed by the twisting of the central pair of blunt-ended feathers. The other two were short tailed and dark brown with light barring underneath indicating immature birds. These scarce passage migrants who breed in Arctic Russia and Spitzbergen were making their way down the east coast of Britain to their wintering grounds off the west coast of Africa. They could obviously sense the rapidly approaching winter as they flew nonchalantly past without any interruption to their flight plans. No sooner had they disappeared behind the sand dunes, held together by a dense thicket of marram grass that acts as a barrier holding back the incoming tide along the entire length of this coastline when another unusual fly-past occurred. As though following the skuas, five very rare geese to this part of the world appeared low over the sandy beach. The white fronted blaze and pinkish bills distinguishing them as white-fronted geese from northern Russia who must have been blown off course from their flight path to winter in eastern England. The Greenland race that winter in the west of Britain have an orange-yellow bill. As with the skua's, one minute they are there the next they are gone. After all that excitement there was just time to reflect on the days observations, enjoy the regular inhabitants once again and say goodbye to Embo - "A Place for Birds".

Chapter 13

ONE OF THOSE MORNINGS

PEREGRINE FALCON

One of the great enjoyments in my life is to take my springer spaniel 'Bracken' for her daily walks. Normally her main long walk takes place in the morning from about 8.45am when there is hardly anyone around and she has a lesser one in the afternoon. This particular morning I had decided to take her on my favourite, if not hers, woodland walk through a mixture of coniferous and deciduous trees to the loch-side. Around where we live she reacts like a typical spaniel running off through the heather and amongst the trees, but away from home territory she tends to stick reasonably close to me with an occasional foray into the undergrowth.

It was early April but due to a late cold snap after a very mild winter (for this part of the world) everything in the natural world was now particularly late. The mildness of the winter had deceived flowers, shrubs and trees to shoot exceptionally early, only having to start again after being cut back with a vengeance by the cold spell. Early migrant birds suddenly found the warm pleasant conditions change overnight to cold, frosty, snow-covered ground with small ponds covered with a thick coating of ice. Many did not survive. The continuous northerly winds that accompanied this unforgiving weather also brought a halt to the migrating geese and swans returning to their breeding grounds in the Arctic. The haunting sight and sounds of skeins of greylags, small flocks of pink feet and whooper swans were therefore much later and continued for much longer than usual.

This cold weather was behind us now and things were beginning to return to normal. As I drove along the single-track road that meandered through the woodland edge, a row buck skipped across the tarmac and disappeared in amongst the willow and birch scrub. Only the sight of his white rump betrayed his continued presence as he looked over his shoulder to check my position before trotting further into the green depths.

I parked my vehicle on the grass verge at the side of the road and as I got out, as if on cue, a willow warbler broke into song. This was the first of the year for me. These small but tough little birds herald the first sound of spring, their sweet wistful song filling the air after a momentous 2,500 mile journey from southern Africa. I'm surprised they have the energy!

As we walked down the small track that leads to the loch the air was punctuated by several willow warblers singing at the top of their voices from the highest vantage points within their territories. Several species of the tit family were flitting in and out of the willow and birch scrub including the delicate and extremely attractive long-tailed variety. This tiny bird is very conspicuous in flight because its long, black edged tail is longer than the length of its body. Being a very small bird they have difficulty in coping with severe winters and many die due to their inability to keep warm. This is one of the bird world's master builders that makes an intricate, oval shaped nest consisting of moss and lichen bound together with cobwebs and lined with feathers, a truly remarkable construction.

The walk to the lochside was uneventful apart from being serenaded by continually increasing numbers of willow warblers, resident robins and wrens plus the very colourful but virtually songless bullfinch. As we climbed up the slope below the towering rock face, Bracken put up yet another woodcock that had been minding its own business camouflaged amongst the heather and russet bracken stalks. This in turn disturbed two very large black and white birds that flew across an opening and clamped onto the bough of a dying but not yet rotten Scots pine tree. They were a breeding pair of great spotted woodpeckers cementing the pair bond by patrolling their territory and checking out suitable nesting sites. The male, whose colourful red nape patch flashed in the morning light, continued to pursue the female around the branches with the occasional stop for a quick drum to claim ownership. The 'drum' is the sound made by eight to ten rapid blows of the bill on a resonant tree delivered within a single sound. Enough to give him a headache!

We continued to make our way along the well trodden path, produced mainly by the tiny feet of foxes and deer, when a sequence of true events took place to gladden the heart, eyes and ears.

As we approached the highest part of the rock face the piercing cry of a peregrine falcon echoed through the canopy of the tall Scots pines. I carefully climbed higher up the slope through a tangled mass of moss-covered scree, partially hidden by dead bracken and fallen Scots pine branches, to a clearing with access to the cliff face. I crouched down next to a deeply fissured old pine tree trunk and called softly to Bracken to join me. Amazingly she obeyed instantly as this male or 'tiercel' flew with a series of shallow flaps, alternated with short glides across the skyline before coming to rest on a lichen-covered boulder. Peregrines are very vocal when not hunting and he was no exception. He continued to call until I saw him peer down from his high vantage point towards my concealed position, alight and disappear over the summit. I know they have good eyesight, but I could not believe he had seen me, then suddenly I realised what had happened. Whilst I was concentrating on this magnificent bird, for I could see every feature - the lightly barred chest, blue/black back and crown, yellow cere to the sharp beak with a dark cheek moustache running down from a yellow eye socket which contained a large brown eye - Bracken had caught a scent and had decided to do a bit of rock climbing as she foraged around the lower ledges in full view. I angrily whistled her back. As she reached my side she squirmed against my leg and looked longingly up into my eyes as if to say - "I'm sorry dad but I couldn't resist the sweet smell of roe deer tracks". The peregrines that nest on a nearby ledge have been very successful over a number of years raising normally two young and occasionally three. The loch appears to be one boundary line of their territory that stretches northwards over miles of heather moorland and rocky outcrops.

Just as we were about to continue the sound of an approaching flock of geese intensified as they got closer until it reached a crescendo as they passed overhead, even making Bracken look skywards. About twenty birds with dark heads and necks with pale bodies appeared creating a musical chorus, as opposed to the farmyard 'honk' of the more usual greylag geese, then disappeared over the trees much too quickly. For these were pink-footed geese that had wintered around here and were now heading for their breeding grounds in Iceland or perhaps Greenland. All the Iceland/Greenland race winter mainly in Scotland (around 90,000 birds) with a few in England, whilst the Spitsbergen population winter in Denmark, western Germany and the low countries. In fact a migration flight line is now known to cross Scotland via the Kyle of Sutherland northwards over Loch Shin and Loch More.

After a further thirty yards of traversing the lower slope of the cliff face a familiar sound echoed around the loch, the red-throated divers had returned. I hurriedly negotiated my descent closely followed by Bracken who, thinking it was a great game, rushed past knocking me off balance and depositing my flailing body amongst the heather. I extracted myself and arrived on the loch-side path rather dishevelled but non-the worst for wear.

Peering through the lower branches of the trees that lined the loch I could see that characteristic uplifted head and deep red throat patch that changed intensity when caught at different angles to the light. There were two swimming a small distance apart when suddenly one extended its neck and emitted a high pitched mewing wail. As if on cue a third bird descended from the sky, aquaplaned along the surface of the water and came to a halt about thirty yards from the agitated pair. At this invasion of their territory both resident birds swam towards the intruder in an aggressive manner. Realising his predicament the intruder 'ran' across the water to gain momentum before flying off towards the head of the loch to a chorus of wails from his adversaries. These were a breeding pair who regularly use this loch to feed on the plentiful supply of fish but nest beside the small, shallow moorland waters to the north and west. Because like all divers their legs are set far back on their bodies to aid propulsion whilst swimming underwater, they have great difficulty in taking off and landing, hence running on water and aquaplaning. But once airborne these ungainly land birds were transformed and circled the loch amid cries of 'kwuk-kwuk-kwuk' before splashing down in unison like ditched sea planes towards the far end of the loch.

I normally take Bracken about half way along the loch to the windy corner before turning back and it was as we were approaching that area that the last phenomenon occurred. All of a sudden Bracken caught a scent and preceded to rush around, nose to the ground, wagging her tail. She tracked down to the waters edge, back across the path and up the hill to where an uprooted tree and fallen boulders had made a natural den and shelter. I follow her to the configuration of stones, branches and dead bracken but could find no evidence of occupancy even though she was sure something had passed that way recently. And her nose is never wrong. With springer spaniels the more you encourage them the more excited they become and reacting to my enthusiasm she again scented across the path to the waters edge and actually into the water itself. Obviously the otters I had previously seen some months back were still frequenting the area and this was confirmed by the fresh spraint (droppings) deposited on the usual large boulder at the windy corner. It was while I was examining the dark slimy faeces containing fish scales and bones that I caught a movement out of the corner of my eye. There flying low across the loch with a slow deliberate wing beat was an osprey. It must have been one of the first to return from its wintering ground in West Africa and could have even been one of the local breeding pair. It did not stay very long and just sailed off effortlessly over the conifer plantation which skirted the far side of the loch. I watched it get smaller and smaller until it disappeared amongst the blue sky and white cumulus clouds. I stood there at the waters edge contemplating the morning's activities and reflecting on how lucky I was to be able to experience those wonderful wonders of nature, when I was suddenly aware of Bracken quietly munching my precious otter droppings. I gently smiled as her actions brought me suddenly back to earth; I know she likes fish but really!

Chapter 14

WOODLAND FEAST

SCOTTISH CROSSBILL

The Loch Fleet Nature Reserve, although managed by the Scottish Wildlife Trust was established by agreement with the joint owners of Cambusmore and Sutherland Estates. The reserve has a wide variety of habitats including pinewoods, sand dunes and the River Fleet estuary, the most northerly inlet on the east coast of Scotland. It is therefore an exciting place to visit at any time of the year especially during early summer when apart from breeding woodland and shore birds, the butterflies and wild flowers that are indigenous to both dunes and pine woods are in abundance.

My journey began at the Mound causeway on the western boundary of the reserve. The Mound was built by Thomas Telford in 1816, to carry the main road north along the coast that had previously run inland from Bonar Bridge to Lairg and down the far side of the River Fleet. Sluice gates were constructed where the river enters the loch to protect the surrounding fields from flooding and to allow salmon to travel from the sea to their spawning grounds. The pressure of the rising tide causes the gates to close and salmon can be seen in the pool below the old bridge waiting for the gates to re-open as the tide recedes. It was hoped that the construction of the causeway would enable the land behind the Mound to be reclaimed for agriculture, but this did not materialise. Gradually this sealed-off area was colonised by alder and willow, extending to 655 acres to become the most extensive alder carr in Scotland. Between the alder wood and the causeway a large tidal lagoon has formed which can be overlooked from a small car park that was reconstructed when the new bridge was built over the river.

It was a pleasant late June day as I drove the Land Rover into the car park to accompany the solitary car already there. As I opened the door I was met with a vaguely familiar song from the gorse and broom bushes on the far side of the car park. I raised my binoculars and the bird disappeared into the bowels of the bush. As usual I thought. I waited for a few minutes for it to re-appear then decided to concentrate on the lagoon. The tide was out in Loch Fleet so there was plenty of mud exposed around the shallow edges and inlets with a wide variety of feeding waders and wildfowl. Towards the back of the lagoon where the water was at its shallowest several species of dabbling duck were concentrated. There were a few pairs of teal, a couple of non-breeding male wigeon, several mallard and a lot of shelduck.

The adult breeding plumage of a very dark green almost black head, white body and rust coloured breast-band of the shelduck contrasted well against the blue-green water and exposed mud banks. This is Britain's' largest duck although it looks, walks and flies like a goose and it is said that this species forms a link between the ducks and geese. Also unlike typical ducks the female does not have drab or inconspicuous plumage but is similar to the drake, only slightly smaller and lacking the knob at the base of the bill. Because of the bright colours of the female they normally nest in either rabbit burrows amongst the sand dunes or under the shelter of bushes or boulders. Every July almost the entire British population of shelduck make for Heligoland Bight off the north-west German coast to moult. Only the juveniles of that year and a few adult females acting as guardians remain to await the return in the autumn. Speaking of juveniles, emerging from some scrub willow and making their way to the waters edge was an early brood of eight endearing ducklings with their parents in attendance. I refer to them as 'humbugs on legs' because of their brown and white striped down resembling the sweets of the same name.

Towards the centre of the shallows moving like clockwork toys were three greenshanks. They were either non-breeders or adults from the adjoining moorlands taking time-out to feed following the change over at the nest site. The greenshank is one of my favourite waders for it is a bird of wild remote country, breeding only in the Highlands, Skye and Outer Hebrides. It differs totally from its near relative the redshank, being larger with an upturned bill and greenish legs. When flying it displays the extensive brilliant white patch stretching from its back through to the rump and tail, which helps to distinguish the species in the wild. These three were feeding at times avocet style, moving their bills from side to side along the surface of the water, then suddenly a contrasting quick dash with neck outstretched in pursuit of small fish just like a heron. The peace of the area was frequently punctuated by the 'twee-wee-wee' call of the common sandpiper as it landed on a fresh area of exposed mud. These small waders along with oystercatchers, curlew and redshank make up the majority of the waders that make use of this rich feeding area. But by far the most numerous bird of the lagoon is the common gull. In spite of its name this bird is by no means the commonest of gulls except in north-west Ireland and Scotland, where Scotland probably holds 80-90% of the British population. In east Sutherland common gull numbers even exceed black-headed, followed by greater black-backed, herring and lesser black-backed. The common gull unlike its relatives is a comparatively demure, quiet and unassuming bird with a very pretty face much like the kittiwakes. In this area they nest on the grassy surrounds between the water and the willow and birch scrub.

Suddenly all hell broke loose! The off-duty and non-breeding gulls rose into the air screaming abuse, ducks were beating the water with their wings like paddle steamers propelling themselves to the safety of the shore and the waders were flying off in all directions. The first thought was a peregrine but above the cloud of gulls was the slow wing beat and stall of a hunting osprey coming into view. Why these birds should be afraid of an osprey whose diet consists of fish only is anyone's guess. I suppose any bird of prey is a threat and potentially dangerous and I also don't expect they have read many bird books. The hunting osprey was flying towards the car park, it occasionally paused and hovered peering into the depths of the lagoon for any sign of a surfacing fish or movement on the sand and shingle bottom. The few ospreys that do inhabit the surrounding area often hunt the sheltered waters of Loch Fleet on the ebb tide in search of a small flatfish called a dab. This particular bird suddenly turned in mid flight and with wings half closed plummeted towards the water, in a split second changed its mind, regained height and continued its flight over the causeway into the heart of the loch.

While all this was happening the small songbird in the gorse bushes had re-appeared to sing its short scratchy song from the top of the yellow flowering bush, this time in full view. A quick glance through the binoculars revealed him in all his splendour. It was a male whitethroat, looking very handsome with his grey head, white throat and chestnut wings. A summer visitor to these shores from central Africa, it is quite common in the south of the country from where I remembered the song. With milder winters and warmer summers warbler numbers in this part of the country have increased but although occasional whitethroats can be seen, the lesser whitethroat has not quite made it over the border.

After this short interesting stop I turned the Land Rover around and headed over the new bridge and on towards the capital town of Sutherland - Golspie. With the statue of the first Duke of Sutherland peering down on me from the heights of Ben Bhraggie, I turned right on the outskirts of the village towards the once small fishing hamlet of Littleferry. Once past the open aspects of the links golf course on the seaward side and the arable fields full of noisy rooks and jackdaws on the other, the single-track road entered a dark corridor enclosed on both sides by conifer plantations. A hundred yards further on a wooden gate and style signalled the start of the Balblair Wood walk.

I parked on the grass verge adjacent to a broken down fence and decided to take only my camera and binoculars as the telescope and tripod can become extremely heavy after a while. The gravel path, which over the years has been covered by invading grasses and mosses, dissects two conifer plantations of different ages. The one on the right many years ago was a plantation of Scots pine but has since been thinned out producing a much more appealing habitat to plants and animals alike. Scots pines tend to lose their bottom branches anyway as they mature but these specimens being originally planted so close together have the appearance of long poles with the occasional bare broken branch and all the greenery confined to the tops. This is the uniform appearance of the part of Balblair Wood that comes within the reserve's boundaries. This phenomenon enables the light to penetrate and the rich undergrowth of ling and bell heather, cross-leaved heath, cowberry and other wild flowers of the pinewood to flourish. The other side of the path, which is not part of the reserve, contains the usual commercial plantation species of sitka spruce and larch, which are of very limited use to wildlife.

Two very rare wild flowers are found in the woodland reserve and are of great interest to the botanical minded. One is the Twinflower (Linnaea Borealis) that is a creeping evergreen with very delicate small pink flowers in pairs and is only found in eastern Scotland. This plant is named after Linnaeus, the man who re-organised botanical naming into the two-name system that we use today. Then there is an even rarer plant found only in a very few locations in northern Scotland. This is the One-flowered Wintergreen (Moneses Uniflora) commonly known as St. Olaf's Candlestick. It has a long stem bearing a solitary creamy-white five petalled flower with a long thick style that gives it the appearance of an upside down candlestick, hence the name. Where St. Olaf, the King of Norway (1015 - 1028) comes in I do not know. In a month's time when these flowers are past their best, the very pretty creeping lady's tresses will begin to poke its head through the thick carpet of heather. This very small-flowered member of the orchid family is common in north-east Scotland but absent elsewhere except East Anglia, Cumbria, Northumberland and south Scotland.

After about 200 yards the path crosses a small burn by way of a wooden slatted bridge. The burn, which started its life on the slopes of Ben Bhraggie, has enabled an open ride to be created between the two conifer plantations as it meanders towards Loch Fleet. Clearings amongst woodlands, either man made or as nature intended, create an ideal habitat for birds and bird watchers alike and this was no exception. As I stood on the bridge I was surrounded by small birds - great tits, blue tits and chaffinches who flitted through the branches of the large beech trees that acted as guardians to the bridge. Small parties of coal tits and siskins flew across the open glade to feed on uneaten cone seeds and robins chased each other through the broom bushes that lined the burn.

The path from this point on had been heavily rutted by forestry machinery when this part of the wood had been thinned out last autumn. This had caused intermittent pools of water to form in the deepest ruts, which are a nuisance to us but act as convenient bird baths to our feathered friends. As I entered the wood a wren burst into its loud melodious song from within a tangle of branch debris and a woodpecker uttered its unmistakable 'tchick-tchick' call from a far off tree.

About 50 yards ahead of me and opposite to a clearing constructed by the forestry as a turning spot for their vehicles were several small birds bathing in a particularly large pool of water. There were chaffinches, the tiny siskins and coal tits with the occasional greenfinch thrown in for good measure. They would fly down to the pool, duck under the water to clean their head and back feathers and then flap their wings vigorously to wash the otherwise unreachable parts. This procedure carried on for several minutes until, looking very bedraggled, they flew to a convenient perch to preen the wet feathers. With this continued succession of birds flying back and forth, I suddenly noticed that a couple of the so-called greenfinches appeared to be larger and greener than the rest. On careful scrutiny and to my great excitement they were female crossbills and judging by the large and stout crossed bill, Scottish crossbills. Then an orange-red plumaged male arrived, then another, followed by further females and several heavily streaked juveniles. What a bonanza! There were about twelve birds in total all having a quick bath and a drink, followed by a forage in the immediate vicinity. Two females and in particular one male, stayed still longer than the others, which allowed me to focus on their outstanding beauty.

Both sexes had dark wings and face patch which contrasted with their bright green and red adult plumage respectively, a forked tail and a large crossed bill, which in all gave them a parrot like appearance. They really are a very striking bird and with maturity their colours become brighter which makes them appear as birds of the tropics, not of the far north. The juveniles are easily recongised by their streaked breast and back. They are totally dependent on regurgitated seed from their parents for about a month after leaving the nest until their bills become crossed. The unusual beak where the upper mandible is straight and the lower is crossed, is designed to extract seeds from pine cones and this is where the physical difference between crossbills becomes apparent. Scottish crossbills have much larger and stouter bills to deal with the much larger cones of the Scots pine and therefore occur mostly in the old native pinewoods of the Highlands. All crossbills are gregarious but Scottish crossbills are seldom seen in parties of more than twenty, whereas common crossbills who principally feed on spruce cones may number up to eighty or a hundred birds. The Scottish crossbill is currently recognised as a distinct species (Loxia Scotica) and is the only British bird that appears nowhere else in the world.

After about ten minutes all the crossbills flew off into the depths of the wood with a distinct 'jip-jip' call as they went. I continued along the track past a stand of half a dozen old beech trees, when the pungent smell of fox stopped me in my tracks. The sudden awareness of a rank 'carnivore' smell will nearly always be due to the strong odour of urine left as a scent mark by a dog fox. The scent marking at this time of year is normally to define boundaries, but during the mating season from December to February the scent changes its composition to attract females.

As I was examining the soft mud on the track for any foxy prints I was distracted by a short scream followed by a rustling noise that appeared to be coming from the rear of the wood that backed onto a grassy field. A large bird clutching something in its talons rose from the ground and alighted onto a nearby branch while I froze in my crouched position. The bird only stayed long enough to secure its grip on its captured prey before flying with great difficulty into the more dense part of the wood. This short pause did though give me sufficient time to identify the bird as a tawny owl that had caught a tiny baby rabbit. This was a very unusual occurrence as tawnies are for the most part nocturnal and rarely take anything larger than a vole. If hard pressed for food at nesting time tawny owls will hunt in broad daylight and judging by the difficulty it had in coping with the excess weight of prey the hungry owlets would at least be satisfied for a few hours.

I continued along the track until I reached another clearing that took the form of a crossroads. Immediately opposite was a track leading to a holiday cottage, whereas the other opposing spurs led to the loch side and back to the main road. On one of the corners of the crossroads the continual use by forestry lorries in the past had created a large indentation, which I had lined with polythene to prevent water seepage, thus enabling the prospective 'bird-bath' to remain longer during dry weather. This had paid off because after concealing myself amongst the undergrowth, the pool was constantly visited by chaffinches, blue and great tits, siskins, greenfinches, coal tits and the very elusive redpoll. In this part of the country redpolls are regularly seen in flight although they invariably land just out of sight but are very often attracted to small pools. The bathing male redpoll was in his adult summer plumage, which is half twite and half linnet. He was basically brown and streaked with a red forehead, pink breast and rump but with a distinctive black chin and buff coloured double wing-bars. It was a real pleasure to observe this bird at close quarters, as it does not happen very often. The most numerous bird at the pool was the siskin, which is often seen in the company of redpolls. This delightful little finch has spread rapidly with the widespread planting of conifers but its main breeding area is still in the pine forests of the Scottish Highlands. These bright yellow and green birds were continually flying to and fro from the pool. The brighter male was particularly striking sporting his black crown and bib compared to the more streaked and less yellow female.

I was concentrating so much on the pool that I nearly missed an added bonus. I was suddenly aware of a movement on the track that eventually leads out to the main road. Standing just in front of a five bar wooden gate, feeding on the grass verge at the edge of the wood was a female (doe) roe deer. She quickly caught my scent and disappeared into the adjoining undergrowth, fluffing out the pale hairs on her rump to form a 'powder puff' as she went. She most probably had a newborn fawn hiding close by amongst the vegetation awaiting her return. Roe deer are the smallest of our native deer and are widespread throughout Scotland but they are difficult to observe because they generally keep to cover and are most active at dawn and dusk. Rutting takes place in July and August but roe deer being the only artiodactyl (hoofed animal) in which delayed implantation of the fertilised egg occurs, does not begin gestation until December and the young are born in the following May or June.

To produce a near circular walk I continued down the left spur of the crossroads for a short distance to emerge on the north shore of Loch Fleet. There were a few waders feeding on the periphery, mainly curlew and oystercatchers with several pairs of shelduck waddling across the exposed wet mud. From here I walked between the edge of the wood and the loch shore that was carpeted with small patches of sea pinks or thrift. As I rounded the corner, where the burn that ran under the wooden slatted bridge flowed into the loch, a pair of mallard rose noisily, quacking their displeasure at being disturbed. Scattered at intervals and growing amongst the grass-covered area between the wood and the burn were clumps of the small white flowered common scurvy grass. This plant has a high content of vitamin C and in the days of sailing ships when voyages often lasted for months, large quantities were taken aboard to prevent the sailors from becoming afflicted with scurvy through their prolonged diet of salt pork and dried biscuits. Despite its name it is not a grass but a member of the cabbage family.

I made my way along the side of the burn where the wet woodland margins were alive with the green-veined white butterfly. This delicate little butterfly who is similar in appearance to the small white but with green streaks that trace the veins on the underwings, deposits its eggs only on wild members of the cabbage family so is therefore not a pest to gardeners. Just before the bridge I disturbed a grey heron that had been feeding on the brown trout fry that inhabited the brown peaty-bottomed burn. The heron's usual flight pattern of a very slow wing beat, neck drawn back and legs trailing beyond the tail, accompanied me on my return to the Land Rover as it made its way to the loch-side shallows.

I drove further along the single-track road for about half a mile until I reached Littleferry, where I pulled into the car park that had been hewn out of the surrounding grass-covered sand dunes. Littleferry, like many of the villages along the east coast of Sutherland, had a small but thriving fishing industry as the still surviving ice house, where the fish were stored before transportation south, bears witness. It was also a centre for the importation of lime and coal for the area and the export of local grain, wool and whisky, but with the opening of the Mound causeway its importance declined. Today the remaining houses are mainly used as holiday cottages with only a few as permanent homes.

This time the telescope and tripod were essential for some sea watching where the coastal path through the dunes ends at the mouth of Loch Fleet. The dune area is criss-crossed with small paths but I had decided to take the higher one that runs along side the channel that leads into the loch. Between the dunes, which were covered in lyme and marram grasses, which help to bind the loose sand, small areas had been colonised by shorter grasses and wild flowers. The flat plateau in the centre of the dune system was covered in a bright yellow carpet of bird's-foot-trefoil, which in turn was decorated by the common blue butterfly. The caterpillar of this particular butterfly feeds on all plants that are members of the pea family, which in this habitat include the vetches and clover as well as the bird's-foot. As I walked further along the path I just had to stop at intervals to examine the small patches of the beautiful tri-coloured wild pansy. It was while I was admiring the purple, yellow and white flowers that a large mottled brown butterfly flew past my face and settled on a solitary thistle that was poking its head above the long grasses. As it folded its wings to drink the nectar, I could see the green suffusion around the silvery spots on the underside of the hind-wing indicating that this was a dark green fritillary, which is predominantly a western species with occasional eastern inroads and most common near the coasts. Other brown butterflies that frequent the dunes include the meadow brown, Britain's commonest butterfly and the small heath. After this great find I continued until just before the end of these dunes to where the open sea comes into view. The path suddenly widened to reveal a floral tribute. The close rabbit cropped grass was covered in a purple, yellow and white profusion of bird's-foot-trefoil, purple milk vetch and wild pansies with barely room to walk past nature's carpet. Strutting through this spectacular sight feeding on the abundance of insects was a pair of skylarks. Several pairs had accompanied me from the car park, performing their conspicuous melodious vertical flight to several hundred feet, hovering, then descending, still sustaining their clear warbling song until they neared the ground. This is how skylarks are usually observed but once on the ground their true identity is revealed. Although basically streaky brown, they appear larger than you would think, with white outer tail feathers and a slight crest that becomes more prominent when the bird is disturbed.

This path ends as the dune system changes to a silver-sand beach that stretches all the way along the coast, past Dunrobin Castle and as far as the eye can see to the Caithness cliffs. With the tide beginning to come in, the resident waders were feeding in earnest amongst the weed-covered rocks that are covered only at high tide. During the summer months there are not the vast numbers of waders normally seen here but oystercatchers, redshank, curlew, dunlin, ringed plovers and a few juvenile bar-tailed godwits managed to sustain my interest. With the aid of the telescope several small groups of eiders, mainly males, could be seen offshore along with a few diving cormorants. Although difficult to see due to the distance involved, a lot of unidentified terns were fishing off a distant sand-bar, these I hoped to have a closer look at further down the coast on another day. I have spent many happy hours here, concealed in the dunes behind the marram grass, watching the tide ebb and flow and the surprises they bring. But it was time to return through the wild garden, back to the Land Rover and home.

Chapter 15

PAST REFLECTIONS

OSPREY

Near to where I live is a narrow glen, which is well renown for its wildlife, particularly birds of prey. I have been privileged to some extraordinary sights that many would give their right arm to see. Obviously all these experiences did not happen on one day so I am therefore going to compile all these together into one chapter, as though it was indeed one day's excursion. All the incidents occurred between the months April to July in reasonable weather apart from one, when the conditions attributed to the proceedings.

The glen is approximately eight miles long with a loch at one end overflowing into a small river, which eventually meanders its way to the sea. The single-track road follows the course of the river from the high moorlands of heather and bracken through to the sparsely covered birch woods of the lower slopes.

I was approaching the last bend in the road before the loch came into view when several small birds flew across my path from one side of the road to the other. Most of these were common meadow pipits that disappeared into the bowels of the heather, but a few birds settled on the wire fence that surrounded a young conifer plantation. As I stopped the Land Rover two of these birds flew to the top of some adjoining tall heather stems and I could see that they were a pair of stonechats. These birds get their name from their call which sounds like two pebbles being struck together. Their close cousin the whinchat gets its name from its preferred habitat of gorse bushes known as 'whins'. Most stonechats stay in Britain all year round and can raise as many as three broods a year to compensate for the high mortality rate during severe winters, whereas the whinchat spends the winter in tropical Africa. The male, who may be paired to more than one female, was letting all and sundry know that this was his territory by being very vocal and also very conspicuous with his striking black head separated from a colourful chestnut breast by a white neck patch.

The loch, although not large, was still of sufficient size for the surface to be disturbed by the gentle breeze, and more significantly as the strength of the wind increased, caused by the funnelling effect of the contours of the surrounding hills. This brisk weather did not appear to bother the red-throated diver that with great difficulty I had spotted fishing on the far side of the loch. The method, as in all divers, is to swim around with the head under the surface to eliminate the glare of the water until a fish is spotted, then to dive in pursuit of the prey. After diving several times, which can be as deep at thirty feet, he decided to call it a day and took off. With rapid wing beats, neck outstretched and legs tucked back, this streamlined and graceful bird flew over the nearest hill towards his breeding moorland lochan.

As I continued along the side of the loch I was accompanied by the 'twi-wi-wi' high pitched call of the common sandpiper as it flew, just above the water, from rock to rock along the edge of the loch. This was a single bird so I expect the female was sitting on her four speckled eggs laid in a scrape of a nest concealed amongst the overgrown vegetation between the loch and the road. The chicks leave the nest as soon as their down is dry, are fully airborne at three weeks old and completely independent at four weeks.

All the way across the moor the road is very narrow with tufts of grass breaking through the cracked tarmac along the unused centre section and sparsely spaced passing places. It was into one of these places, near the very end of the loch, that I dived into and screeched to a halt as I saw a very large bird heading towards me. It proceeded to land half way up one of the electricity pylons between the loch and a very young conifer plantation. These pylons that stretch right across the moorland, although an eyesore, do act as a convenient observation perch for a number of raptor species. Through my binoculars I could see that it was an osprey that was continually being harassed by several meadow pipits. He (I assumed it was a male as both sexes are alike) appeared to ignore this intrusion for he was more interested in other things. He then took off, flew right over my head and circled over the centre of the loch at about a hundred feet above the water. He circled twice descending gradually until when at about sixty feet he began to hover like a kestrel. The stiff breeze had caused small white horses to cover the loch, which made it extremely difficult for the osprey to spot any large fish near the surface, but this bird was hungry. He dropped a further twenty feet, hovered momentarily, then with wings half closed plummeted into the water feet first. He emerged with a large sea trout in his talons and after adjusting his grip on the fish, shook his plumage violently to remove the excess water. He carried the fish torpedo style over the road and landed on one of the large round strainer posts that made up part of the fencing around the conifer plantation. I quickly got out the telescope as he began to feed. Normally with a breeding pair, the male, after a successful plunge, eats the head himself and flies back to the nest with the remains of the fish. This bird was obviously unattached for although starting at the head he continued to eat with relish his prize he had worked so hard for. I have seen many ospreys in the years I have been birdwatching in the Highlands, but apart from on film this was the first time I had observed the entire scene of a successful dive. Tearing myself away from the feeding osprey I had to chuckle to myself as I could see at the far end of the loch four anglers struggling with the elements, completely oblivious to the technique of the master at work. Much has been said about the famous nest site at Loch Garten in Speyside, but there are a few in Sutherland, one of which I have had the pleasure of watching for many years. This particular nest, which in common with many, sits precariously on top of a dead Scots pine tree, has had mixed success over the last ten years. Initially the problem was with egg collectors, but this has been virtually eradicated by the vigilance of locals acting as nest watchers around the clock. For the first few years with this protection two or three young were reared on a regular basis, but since then success has been patchy. There are many reasons for this, for when a regular breeding pair is broken up through death or old age, it takes time for the next generation to establish itself. Inexperienced males or females, disturbance by other ospreys and bad weather at the wrong time, can cause breeding failure, but with luck our local ospreys will add to the continuing success achieved by ospreys in general throughout their breeding range. Although seen on film many times, nothing can compete with the experience of being out in the wilds watching a male circle over the nest site with a headless fish gripped in his talons before being encouraged down by the shrilling call of the impatient female; to watch him fly to a nearby branch to preen after depositing the fish into the nest for the female to tear off small pieces and delicately feed the two or three hungry chicks, who after a lengthy eight weeks, grow into magnificent fish hawks. In October these youngsters along with others will migrate to the Gambia in West Africa, where they will spend the next two years before returning to Scotland every spring to eventually breed at five years of age.

Just after the loch the road climbs high above the meandering river and it is here that I have had my best views of Britain's smallest raptor, the merlin. Alas, after several years of breeding success this resident pair disappeared and I have not seen them since. My first encounter began when I spotted a bird flying low over the heather across the upward slope of the hill just beyond the river, so I pulled onto the grass verge to obtain a more detailed look. Imagine my surprise when the bird suddenly appeared and landed right in front of me on a flat topped lichen covered boulder, clutching a meadow pipit in its talons. This female then proceeded to first pluck the breast feathers of the unfortunate pipit before tearing at the exposed flesh with her hooked beak. The female is larger than the male with a dark brown back and a banded tail, whereas the mistle thrush size male has a slate blue back and tail which has a black band. Merlins, once the falconry bird of noblewomen, are quite rare with probably only 600-800 pairs in the whole of the UK. After a few mouthfuls she flew down towards the river and presented the remains to a well developed brown streaked youngster who was perched on the frame of a disused crow trap. To my astonishment she was joined by two more young and the male could be seen perched on top of a riverside willow tree standing guard over the proceedings. These crow traps are large wood and mesh cages where the top mesh is constructed into the shape of a funnel. When the crows descend into the baited cage through the open funnel, they are unable to escape back through the small neck of the funnel and are subsequently shot by the keeper. This is common practice at lambing time to control the predatory instincts of hooded and carrion crows. The following year I was again privileged as I rounded a slight bend in the road in the same area. There, trying to balance on a very thin bendy rowan tree sapling was a very speckled young merlin who virtually used the bonnet of the Land Rover to assist his passage from his precarious perch to the moorland below the road. Having crash dived into the heather and scrambled onto a prominent boulder, this newly fledged bird and two further siblings who were ensconced on further large rocks, were continually supplied with prey by both male and female during my hourly vigil. To observe a whole family of merlins at such close quarters and for such a length of time stands out as one of the finest highlights of my birdwatching life.

The following year a pair of peregrines decided to nest on an adjacent rocky outcrop, which was probably what made the merlins move to pastures new. The peregrines had two successful years before also disappearing but this was due to human disturbance as the nest site was easily accessible and close to the road. I first discovered this nest site when I was studying a hunting male hen harrier quartering the upper heights of the hill far above the river. As if on cue, as the harrier disappeared over the top of the hill, the screams of the approaching adult falcon pierced the silence. After about half an hour of retracing my steps and scouring every rock face I eventually located the eyrie, or should I say located the chicks. The nesting depression itself was lying well back from the cliff edge behind a substantial clump of heather, which not only hid the chicks from view but also disguised the white guano splashings. It wasn't until the chicks in their white fluffy down became restless and started to move around that they themselves became apparent. I counted three heads. I continued to periodically monitor their progress right through to fledging but when they were ringed only two of the smaller males were found in the nest, indicating that one, most probably a female, had been stolen. The larger and fiercer females are prized by falconers and this violation was most probably a contributing factor to the fact that the parents did not nest within the area again. The problem with peregrines is that they are so vocal on approaching and defending their nesting area that they are easily detected. Their only defence is the inaccessibility of the nest site itself as chicks and eggs are stolen for falconry and monetary gain and added to this some gamekeepers still destroy the birds in defence of red grouse. Although illegal this fate is suffered by both the peregrine and hen harrier that are blamed for the decline in grouse numbers by estate owners. It is admitted that these birds do affect numbers when grouse breeding success is affected by bad winters or disease, but a healthy, well managed grouse population can only be complimented by these magnificent natural predators.

It was from this vantage point high above the river that I saw my first otter since moving from the north-west coast of Highland region where they are in abundance. Generally in the north-east of Sutherland they are mainly nocturnal, but on this particular day the weather was more akin to the west coast, horizontal rain, dull with low mist swirling around even the lowest of the hills. Suddenly my passenger casually remarked, "look a water vole". Being fifty feet above the river I was amazed at her eyesight, until following her precise directions I saw her alleged water vole. Her perception of size at a distance is a common problem for people not used to being in wide open spaces. Many town dwellers never see deer grazing on a distant hillside as their mind and eyes find it difficult to adjust to the size of far off objects. This eight inch water vole was in fact a thirty six inch otter. The male or dog otter has a heavier head and thicker neck than the slightly smaller female (bitch) but from a distance gender was difficult to ascertain. The otter was working its way upstream searching every nook and crannie of the shallow river for any unsuspecting fish. After several forays in an occasional deep pool this otter took a short diversion through the heather, by-passing a sweeping bend before disappearing back into the river again. As it crossed the open ground the contrast between the running, hunched almost comical rolling gait and the graceful movement of its streamlined body as it explores its watery world was remarkable. I have seen several tracks of otters in the mud and sand of the many small inlets around the lochside but this was the first sighting to date.

This particular area of the moors has been quite a success story for studying one of the UK's rarest of raptors, the hen harrier. The female, who resembles a buzzard but has longer wings and a distinctive white rump, builds a nest of grass and bracken in a bare scrape on the ground amongst mature moorland heather. The male, with his contrasting pale grey plumage, white rump and black wing tips, is the easiest of the two to spot as he quarters his moorland habitat. Not only have I been privileged to see these magnificent birds of prey on a regular basis but I have also witnessed the spectacular manoeuvre common to most harriers, the food pass. This occurs when the female greets the male as he brings food for her and the chicks. I was driving across the moors one late spring day when a male suddenly appeared on the left side of the road, having descended from a small gully that dissected the distant hill. He flew across the road towards a large electricity pylon and veering to the right began to hover about thirty feet above the heather. The next sequence of events happened in seconds. After being called, the unseen female rose from the nest, rolled over and caught the prey that the male had dropped to her in her talons, rolled back and returned to the camouflaged nest site. The male then continued on his way, searching the surrounding moorland for further small mammals to supply his insatiable brood. A truly memorable moment to savour. Now that the persecution of hen harriers has again reached intolerable heights, the RSPB has resorted to wing-tagging the young for identification purposes in their research campaign. These large brightly coloured tags do give the birds limited protection but many are still shot or poisoned.

Another ground nesting raptor of these parts is the short-eared owl. The great thing about this bird is that it is diurnal, that is it hunts during the daylight hours enabling it to be seen more readily, unlike other British owls. Many short-eared owls desert their breeding range in the winter months and fly south to the wetlands and marshlands of England before re-appearing in early spring on the treeless countryside of Scotland and northern England. On one such occasion I was driving through the moorland on a pleasant April evening when this large stocky bird with wing-beats like those of an enormous moth flew high across the single track road. I realised it was a short-eared owl by its long barred wings with dark patches at the wrist, short body, large round head and pale underparts. As I approached a sharp bend that took the road down to the riverside, a convenient passing place beckoned. I stopped the Land Rover and looked back towards the area of moorland, now in the shadow of the setting sun, where the owl was beginning his display flight. I watched as he flew, then glided in large circles, eventually dropping his wings below his body and making a loud clapping noise with his wing tips as if he was pleased with his choice of breeding territory. After a short while he was joined by the female who rose from a clump of heather in front of a large boulder. The male continued to display with low zigzag flights and more wing clapping until the female returned to the selected nest site. The male then flew off towards an adjacent young conifer plantation, where he hunted the periphery for an unsuspecting vole to present to the female in order to cement the bond between them. The short-eared owl, like the hen harrier, relies largely on the short-tailed vole and if this food supply is curtailed by a large drop in numbers due to the voles breeding cycle or the continued planting of conifers across the open moorland, then these birds can be severely affected.

Opposite the passing place is a large vertical sand bank that rises abruptly from the shingle bed that follows the natural curve of the river. Just below the peat and heather covered top, small holes have been excavated by the appealing sand martin. These horizontal tunnels are dug out by the birds using their feet and are between two and three feet long with the end enlarged to form a nesting chamber. It is a real pleasure to stand and watch these relatively rare visitors to northern Scotland as they twist and swoop over the river and adjoining moorland feeding on insects, uttering their hard twittering call. The adult sand martin is easily identified in flight by a brown band across its white breast and all brown upper parts, as opposed to its cousin the house martins blue/black livery and white rump. The sand martins numbers plummeted a few years ago with the effects of a prolonged drought in Africa (its winter quarters) and the sand bank was virtually deserted, but since then the numbers have thankfully gradually increased.

After the road descends from the moors it passes through birch, willow and alder woodlands, before an even smaller road to the right rises abruptly to a hamlet of two or three crofts. It was on one day during mid-summer that I was driving along this narrow track, past the contrasting dilapidated farm buildings and neat newly painted cottages, towards a small lay-by that overlooks a large area of alder and willow scrub. Several diversions were needed around sheep dozing in the sunshine, free-range chickens scurrying about and numerous baby rabbits running from the noise of the vehicle. Nesting swallows continually swooped low over the track before accurately negotiating small openings that led into the rusty corrugated iron roofed stone byres that lined the road. As I was admiring the panoramic view that spread before me, stretching from the beginning of Loch Fleet, across the scrub, and through the glen to the village of Rogart, I was suddenly aware of two birds engaged in an aerial dogfight. On further inspection it wasn't a fight but appeared to be a rather robust game between two juveniles, a peregrine and a raven. Both were raised in the area, the raven on the rock face behind me and the peregrine further down the glen. They are both very aerobatic but the peregrine has the edge on manoeuvrability, rightly earning the reputation as the ultimate flying machine. After several minutes of playing tag and follow my leader the peregrine obviously decided I should become part of the game. Having disappeared behind my line of sight I was startled by a sudden rush of air past my ear as the peregrine buzzed me, before climbing steeply into the blue sky to continue the confrontation with the raven who was becoming bored with the situation. Several aerobatic manoeuvres later by the young peregrine on the rapidly disappearing raven resulted in the peregrine suddenly folding his wings back, as in the infamous 'stoop', and diving across the glen like an arrow at a phenomenal speed to disappear into the distance. Juvenile peregrines often carry on like this to develop their flying and hunting skills but normally with their own siblings, and this is the only time I have seen two juveniles of different species act together in this way.

This particular stretch of road has throughout the years enabled me to experience many different and exciting phenomenon (of which these episodes are but a few) that have enhanced my knowledge of the natural world.

Printed in the United Kingdom
by Lightning Source UK Ltd.
134374UK00002B/58-63/P

9 781434 396471